THE HUMAN CHURCH
IN THE PRESENCE OF CHRIST

THE HUMAN CHURCH IN THE PRESENCE OF CHRIST

The Congregation Rediscovered

BY
VICTOR L. HUNTER
AND PHILLIP JOHNSON

 MERCER
UNIVERSITY PRESS

ISBN 0-86554-171-X

The Scripture quotations in this publication from the Revised Standard Version (RSV) of the Bible are copyrighted 1946, 1952, ©1971, 1973 by the Division of Christian Education of the National Council of Churches of Christ in the U.S.A., and are used by permission.

All books published by Mercer University Press are printed on acid-free paper that exceeds the minimum standards set by the National Historical Publications and Records Commission.

Library of Congress Cataloging in Publication Data
Hunter, Victor L., 1942–
    The human church in the presence of Christ.
    Includes index.
    1. Church. I. Johnson, Phillip, 1950–   II. Title.
BV600.2.H86   1985   262'.2   85-11463
ISBN 0-86554-171-X (alk. paper)

CONTENTS

75964

Contents

One generation shall laud thy works to another,
and shall declare thy mighty acts.

Psalm 145:4

FOR OUR PARENTS
Russell and Gwen Hunter
and
Max and Joy Johnson
and
FOR OUR CHILDREN
Heather, Charisa, and Lance
and
Alison, Meghan, Nathan, and Thomas

For where two or three are gathered in my name,
there am I in the midst of them.

Matthew 18:20

PREFACE

Eric Hoffer, the longshoreman/philosopher, was fond of talking about the importance of asking questions. Social stagnation, he observed, was a result of the absence of the impulse to ask questions. Asking questions in light of experience is the starting point for every discovery, every step forward, in the human journey. When Jesus was asked, "What shall I do to inherit eternal life?" he responded by asking the inquirer two more questions.

During the winter of 1978 the impulse to ask questions about our own lives, ministries, and churches seemed urgent to us. Nearly twenty years of pastoral experience between us in small, urban churches in Atlanta, London, New York, and Trenton had left us with far more questions than answers. Yet it was a time when the church had recoiled in a backlash from the 1960s and wanted exclamation marks, not question marks. These exclamation marks were being given in the language of church growth and church management, in an increased "professionalism" among the clergy, and in more frantic activity in church bureaucracy.

Though the time was not conducive to the asking of questions, still they persisted. The questions were deeply personal, for we had come to feel a deep dissatisfaction with our own response to the challenge of the gospel and its call to discipleship and to a life-transforming and joyful spirituality. We were also concerned about our failure to lead our churches into a deeper experience of Christian community in the contemporary urban context.

From one perspective the questions appeared to be ecclesiological. What is the future of the urban church in light of its current structures, values, and theological underpinnings? Does the central Christian narrative shape the identity of the local congregation, or do the dominant cultural values? Do the forms the church takes today correspond in any way to the essence of the meaning of Christian community in the New Testament? How does the congregation experience the "holy" and the "transcendent" in its own life, and how are these realities mediated in our secular world? What is the place and purpose of Christian worship in such a context? Does evangelism have any meaning or integrity any more? Have the familiar forms and habits of Christian fellowship cut us off from any meaningful contact with the "least of these" whom Christ indwells? What, in fact, does it mean to "be church?" The New Testament reverberates with the confidence that the church—even in powerlessness—can be a true sign of the new humanity and an effectual avenue of Christ's presence in the world. Can we today find that confidence and claim that presence?

From another perspective our questions were simply the deep human questions we all share—questions about values, meaning, loneliness, anxiety, freedom, love, play, suffering, justice, death. How do we keep human life human and celebrate the gift of life in the midst of contradictions and ambiguity?

With the doctrine of the Incarnation as a theological starting point, we understood these questions as belonging to a single reality. And since they were both existential and theological questions, we felt they were questions that needed to be "lived." Our attempt to "live" the questions set us on a journey that in turn led us to draw together a pilgrim community in inner London known as Disciples House. In 1979 our families moved into a redundant Anglican vicarage in London's Borough of Camden. We were joined in 1981 by Eric and Debi Greer. Over the past six years Disciples House has evolved into a grassroots, ecumenical Christian community involving some sixty people. Our backgrounds are varied—Roman Catholic, Anglican, Methodist, Baptist, Church of Christ. We have sought to understand the nature of Christian community and the practice of Christian ministry in the city. We have worked with a number of local churches of various traditions and have housed visitors from England, Europe, Africa, India, and South and North America.

Disciples House has found itself inexorably drawn to bound-
ary situations that have become gaps of separation within many
churches today—gaps between clergy and laity, believer and non-
believer, the "insider" and the "outsider," the housed and the
homeless, the citizen and the sojourner, the rich and the poor, the
institutionalist and the anti-institutionalist, the educated and the
uneducated, the political activist and the religious pietist, to name
but a few. During these years we have struggled as never before to
hold together theory and practice, reflection and action.

These essays were born out of our experience. It is our hope
that this book will enhance in some small way a broad ecumenical dialogue-in-living about the mission and ministry of the
Christian community. Even more, we hope it will provide theological and practical foundations for the question-living that is
going on at the local congregational level. A part of what has happened to us at Disciples House is a deepening of our commitment
to the local congregation, but to the congregation as it is infused
with the broad and deep, truly catholic spirit of the Christian faith.
The ecumenical must not despise the local; the local must not be
reduced to the parochial.

It is this creative tension between the ecumenical and the local, the universal and the particular, the catholic and the congregational, that we hope breathes through these reflections. This is
the inherent tension in our faith; it flows from the Incarnation,
when the universally present God embraced the local and particular in Jesus of Nazareth. It is a tension that is vital for ecclesiology in our time. "Church renewal" can never mean anything less
than the renewal of our humanity in the universal humanity of
Christ.

We must all be prepared for surprises in the answers we find
and in the new questions those answers will generate. In the pages
that follow we have tried to explicate our belief that efforts to find
the answers should lead us toward canon, community, and communion.

No book, of course, is simply the product of the author's own
thought. We have tried to acknowledge in our notes the sources
that have informed our thought. Through many years of study and
preaching we are certain we have absorbed more than we recog-

nize from professors who have taught us, colleagues who have worked with us, and writers who have been our daily companions. No oversight is intended; we can only plead that their influence has become a part of us.

Beyond that, there are those we wish to thank for their direct contribution to this endeavor. The members of the Disciples House community and all those who have supported it through the years have provided challenge, insight, and encouragement and have been our traveling companions in the way. Particularly, our colleague and fellow pastor, Eric Greer, has read, questioned, criticized, and encouraged throughout the writing process. His graceful willingness to assume extra duties from time to time in order to free us to write is typical of his supportive and generous spirit. We are grateful also to David Balch, Stratford Caldecott, James Galuhn, James Hulsey, Thomas Hurcombe, and George Stroup for their insights and criticisms. They are responsible only for their friendship and willingness to criticize these essays from the perspective of their varied traditions and disciplines as Protestant pastors, systematic and New Testament theologians, Anglican priests, and Roman Catholic and Protestant lay leaders and community workers. They are not responsible for any shortcomings of this book.

We are indebted to Everett Ferguson for permission to use his translations of the early fathers at the beginning of each chapter (*Early Christians Speak* [Abilene TX: Abilene Christian University Press, 1984]) and to *Mission Journal* and its editor, Bobbie Lee Holley, for permission to use material that has appeared there in a different form.

Finally, a special word of gratitude is due our wives, Lynette Hunter and Janet Johnson, who have shared and endured with grace and wit not only our writing of this book but the many years of the stresses and strains of our pastoral ministries.

Victor L. Hunter
Phillip Johnson

Disciples House
London, England
Epiphany 1985

PART I

WHERE TWO OR THREE ARE GATHERED IN MY NAME

1

THE PRIMACY
OF THE
CONGREGATION

*You are to come together in one place and seek the
common good.*

Epistle of Barnabas

*T*his is a book about the Christian congregation, about
being together in the name of Jesus Christ. It is about worshiping
and working and thinking and suffering together in his presence.
We pretend no exhaustive or systematic prescription. What we
offer instead is a series of reflections, at some points meditations,
that are bound very tightly to our time and place—to our urban,
largely secular society in the late twentieth century.

We want to affirm the possibility of a joyful, graceful, and vigorous life, a life that is a sign of Christ in the places where we live.
Such life, wherever it is born and sustained, is the gift of God; but
it is a gift that is a task, a work to be done. It is a work we want to
do and are trying to do.

We are vividly aware that such affirmations must be made in conscious tension with some very stark truths about our own lives and the lives around us. These truths include

- the suffering of many; the emotional, physical, and spiritual suffering that is only feebly hidden by the apparent ease of our lives and that persists in spite of the progress we often praise.
- the loneliness that often intensifies suffering; the isolation and rootlessness and the absence of friendship in the lives of many.
- the expansion of greed that is idolatry and that so quickly destroys human community, but that nevertheless tempts even the best of people.
- the anxiety of life lived under the shadow of great destructive power and the craving for security.
- the sense of powerlessness and paralysis and the loss of the capacity to give ourselves to good work at the cost of some sacrifice.
- the huge gap that separates the well-to-do from the others for whom life is hard and painful.
- the chasm that separates belief from unbelief, a chasm that renders meaningless much that goes by the name of evangelism.
- the growing domination of technique over our lives, the absence of the awareness of mystery and meaningful reflection, the mistrust of wisdom.

There is, of course, nothing new about suffering, alienation, anxiety, greed, unbelief, or the threat of destruction. It may be true, as many say, that these sins and afflictions are taking on fearful dimensions in our modern life. What we know is that each of us labors under these burdens. They form a backdrop to the work of building Christian communities and lend a certain urgency to the task.

The formation of the Christian congregation has become increasingly difficult in the industrial-technocratic world in which Freud wondered whether it might not be impossible after all to form any kind of community. . . . The increasing coldness of human life, the increasing inability to feel with others and thus to form communal relationships, is the most ominous threat to the human future in Western society. For without the formation of communities there can be no solutions to the dehumanization which is taking place in the political, economic, cultural, and natural dimensions of life.[1]

This statement sets the meaning of the congregation against a very large vista of "the human future in Western society." The relation of Christian communities to the wider society is certainly critical. But as Meeks's statement implies, phrases like "the human future in Western society" remain frail abstractions if our thought does not take root in the concrete and the personal dimensions of our lives. Thus we hope that our reflections are alive with the paradox of the universal in the particular: that our lives can move outward only as they can penetrate inward toward the deepest personal life; that our love can reach out universally only as it finds depth in the love of persons; that our churches can serve the world only as they are fired by a deep-running interpersonal communion within.

THE PERSON

Some years ago a member of the British Coal Board said the most important product to come out of the British coal mine is the person. The human dimension in this rugged and dangerous work was often lost in the production demands of an industry vital to the nation's economy. Working conditions and safety standards were sometimes neglected for more pressing economic goals. In short, the welfare of the person was submerged beneath important but secondary concerns. This did not occur deliberately or with malice. It simply happened under the stress and strain of one industry's set of priorities.

Such forgetfulness often marks the life of the church. We forget that the most important "product" to come out of the church is the person in his or her healing, wholeness, and redemption. It does not occur deliberately or maliciously in the church, either;

---

[1]M. Douglas Meeks, introduction, in Jürgen Moltmann, *The Open Church* (London: SCM Press, 1978) 13, 16-17. This book was originally published as *The Passion for Life* (Philadelphia: Fortress Press, 1978).

but too often our goals, plans, programs, and agendas drop the person below the sightline of concern. When this happens we have exchanged the mystery of ministry to persons by persons in the presence of the Three-Person God for the predictable manipulation of the members of the organization.

C. S. Lewis poignantly touched this theme in some words he wrote into the flyleaf of his copy of Baron von Hügel's *Eternal Life.*

> It is not an abstraction called Humanity that is to be saved. It is you . . . your soul, and, in some sense yet to be understood, even your body, that was made for the high and holy place. All that you are . . . every fold and crease of your individuality was devised from all eternity to fit God as a glove fits a hand. All that intimate particularity you can hardly grasp yourself, much less communicate to your fellow creatures, is no mystery to him. He made those ins and outs that he might fill them. Then he gave your soul so curious a life because it is the key designed to unlock that door, of all the myriad doors in him.[2]

All the "ins and outs" of the suffering, needs, longings, and questions of the person's life must give shape to the church's life and ministry. In the presence of the Good Shepherd of the soul these human realities, in all their depth and complexity, are not to be lost in religious propositions and ecclesiastical programs.

In our Christian experience some of us are more adept at listening to the ancient stories of Abraham and Sarah, Moses and Miriam, Mary and Peter, than we are in attending to the "stories" of the brothers and sisters we live with every day. We may have never even listened to our own heartbeat or given our own experience enough authority for there to be a genuine meeting between our own personal identity and the biblical story. Life with God then becomes a vicarious existence in the then and there of the biblical world rather than a creative and responsible pilgrimage in the here and now of our own world. Rabbi Zusya illumi-

---

[2]Quoted by Eugene Peterson in *Five Smooth Stones for Pastoral Work* (Atlanta: John Knox Press, 1980) 63, and taken from Corbin Scott Carnell, *Bright Shadow of Reality: C. S. Lewis and the Feeling Intellect* (Grand Rapids MI: Eerdmans, 1974) 163.

nated this concern when he said upon nearing death, "In the world to come I shall not be asked: 'Why were you not Moses?' I shall be asked: 'Why were you not Zusya?' "[3] Your own life is the key that unlocks your door to "all the myriad doors in him."

This does not mean that all you do is "right" or that your personal experience becomes normative in opposition to the biblical story. But it does mean that your experience must count as real, in its "good" and "bad" parts. If you fail to pay attention to the truth of your own experience there can be no genuine intersection with the gospel and the tradition in such a way that God's revelation becomes authentically illuminating for you in the present. There must be a genuine encounter between the "I am" of your own existence and the "I Am" of God as revealed through history.

Thus, to write a book about the Christian congregation is not to forget the Christian person. But to speak knowingly about the person means that we must speak with the very next breath about the community. Christianity knows well the adjective "personal," but "private" is a foreign word; the Christian spirit is intimately acquainted with the individual but is a complete stranger to individualism. My life as a person can find wholeness only as I am shaped and reshaped by my encounter with others. Only as the inner estrangement that is the burden of our sin is penetrated by the persistent, often painful, but loving presence of others can I find my true identity in God. This mutual loving and suffering presence is the mystery of the Christian community. It is a mystery founded in God, who in the trinitarian fellowship of Father, Son, and Holy Spirit, is the eternal and perfect community from which "every family in heaven and on earth takes its name" (Eph. 3:15).

THE COMMUNITY

There is, then, no such thing as a solitary Christianity (though there is, of course, a genuine Christian solitude that can be the seed of deeper community). When the voice of Jesus was first heard in

---

[3]Martin Buber, *The Way of Man* (Secaucus NJ: Citadel Press, 1966) 17.

that original call "Follow me," those who answered found themselves bound together in a new form of shared life. Their discovery of the Messiah was at the same time a discovery of a new self-identity in communion with others. The ethic of Jesus in the Gospels pushes relentlessly toward a new sharing of all life's resources.

When the spirit of Pentecost burned in the lives of those first newly baptized Christians, there came a shattering experience of community—a new gladness, a new giving, a new hospitality (Acts 2:42-46). In the Epistles to the young churches all matters, from prayer to economics, are considered in the context of the communion of Christians. The watchword was "welcome one another as Christ has welcomed you" (Rom. 15:7).

The very language of the New Testament betrays this persistent communal assumption. For example, the word *hagios* (saint) is never used to refer to an individual member of the church but often to the local Christian congregation.[4] The sanctifying work of God, God's work of making persons holy, is at the same time a community-making work. Holiness implies the new love of the new community.

This community of Christ means a unity of God that stretches in human history from Abraham into all the generations of the faithful yet to come. To be a member of this community means to be joined in a worldwide society of men, women, and children of every race. This consciousness of communion across the ages and around the globe needs desperately to be renewed, especially in the Protestant churches where it has been so neglected. And yet, can that word church signify anything real to us if it does not first speak of an immediate, concrete form of community where life is nourished at the most intimate level?

The word church has had to do such heavy duty, describing so many different levels of Christian life, that it has come to mean very little to many Christians. We speak of the ideal, invisible church; the denominational church with its bureaucracy; the state or national church. In these days of mass media we have even

---

[4]Two unlikely exceptions are Rev. 20:6 and 22:11.

come to think in terms of "mega-church," the "T.V. church," or the "electronic church." While each of these concepts is descriptive and has more or less merit, each is still what we might call the church at arm's length.

We would like to argue again for the essential and central place of the congregation in our understanding of the church. "Where two or three are gathered in my name," said Jesus, "there am I in the midst of them" (Matt. 18:20). We want to speak a word to and on behalf of the congregation as a gathered people—the *ecclesia*—that local, perhaps very small and powerless gathering of men, women, and children. How in our small places and out of our powerlessness can we gather in Christ's name for the renewal of life? How can such communities function as a living *body* while maintaining the significance of the unique gifts and burdens of the individual? How can the single person be held sacred without splintering the wholeness of the fellowship into a collection of individuals who simply dip into the church's life in whatever way happens to suit them?

The various Christian traditions proffer various theological statements about the church; they interpret our Christian history in differing and often conflicting ways. But all theologies of the church must finally test their truth against the particular demands of the local fellowship. Especially in this concern we do not live by theory alone. Just because we hold dear the universal church of Jesus Christ, we must commit ourselves to the local community. After all, it is in bearing with one another within the local community—bearing our moods, our idiosyncrasies, our sins, our diversities, our varied thoughts and personalities—that our *being* church either thrives or founders. If we do not actually experience the church on the level of the local and particular, the universal church becomes a remote "item" of the dogma.

It is too easily forgotten that the church is not simply an institution that gains fullness and wholeness by virtue of size. In fact, after centuries of organization and expansion, Protestants and Catholics alike still acknowledge (at least in official statements) that the local church, the congregation, is not merely a province or fragment of the larger church. As Hans Küng has plainly written, "The local church is the church and can fully represent the cause of Jesus Christ."[5] This is true because the church is the church of Jesus Christ by virtue of its being the sign of Christ in the world. In other words, the church is not *primarily* an institutional reality; it is a sacramental reality. It is a sign and bearer of the presence of Jesus Christ who has promised to be "in the midst" of his *ecclesia*.

It would be easy to miss the startling implications of this affirmation. It declares that a genuine Christian presence in the world does not depend for its mission on any sort of collective power, influence, manipulation, or control. It means that the Christian community is empowered to emulate its Lord in the renunciation of power for the way of powerlessness that is a part of the strange logic of love. Here lies the source of courage to be the church of Christ in the small place of the congregation.

Sometimes an emphasis on the quality of fellowship in the church is falsely opposed to the deepening of the spiritual and sacramental life of the church. But we insist that the building of the congregation demands that Protestant churches ought to become more, not less, sacramental in thought and practice. A deepening in our sacramental thinking ought to entail a sacramental vision of the *human fellowship of the church*, which is filled by the spirit of Jesus Christ. This loving fellowship, Christ says, stands as a sacrament of God to the world—"that they may be one; even as thou Father, art in me, and I in thee . . . that the world may believe that thou hast sent me" (John 17:21). This text is often read in a broad ecumenical context, and rightly so. Still, if the oneness for which Jesus prayed is not first a living concrete fellowship where person meets person, ecumenism is reduced to a mere formalism.

This is why it is right to insist on the primacy of the local fellowship in our concern for the integrity of the church's life. As Jürgen Moltmann has written,

The church will not overcome its present crisis through reform of

---

[5]Hans Küng, *On Being a Christian*, trans. E. Quinn (Garden City NY: Doubleday, 1976) 480.

the administration of the sacraments, or from reform of its ministries. It will overcome this crisis through the rebirth of practical
fellowship. The reforms of evangelization and administration of
the sacraments, and the inescapable reform of the churches' ministries will spring from the rebirth of fellowship and friendship
among the rank and file.[6]

This focus on the local fellowship does not imply for us, as it seems
to do for Moltmann, an automatic judgment in favor of one given
church polity over another—for "congregational" over "episcopal," or for "low" over "high" forms of government and polity.
Even a brief glance across the spectrum of Christian traditions reveals very quickly that clerical domination and the absence of
genuine community are hardly the prerogatives of the "hierarchical" churches. The scene is full of paradox. But the weariness
with reform "from the top" that Moltmann's statement exhibits is
surely felt by many of us in the church. We have come to doubt
the efficacy of reform and renewal which is not met by the genuine renewal of life at the most fundamental level.

Is it realistic to speak with such hope about the Christian congregation? What, after all, has been our experience in our congregations? All of us from time to time have found ourselves disposed
toward the church as Charlie Brown is toward people: "I love humanity, it's people I can't stand." We love the church; it's the local congregation we find so difficult.

Most of us have mixed feelings about our experience in local
congregations. There have been bright tones and dark shades. After
all, the congregation in some shape or form has been the cradle of
our faith. There we first learned the biblical story. There we made
our first commitment to Christ and found some nourishment along
the way. For most of us congregations have been the scenes of
countless small kindnesses. Some of us have found rare friendships and love even in our sins and troubles. We would be fools
to discount such light in our pasts.

---

[6]Jürgen Moltmann, The Church in the Power of the Spirit, trans. Margaret Kohl (London: SCM Press, 1977) 317.

But no amount of gratitude for such Christian pasts as we have received can gloss over the disappointment and even bitterness engendered by the failure of love and vision in Christian congregations. The chasm that separates the ideal church of our faith and proclamation from the real church of our experience has grown so wide we can barely see across it. For too long we have had to hide our deepest hurts, our most burdensome sins, our real and certain gifts, so that we have come to feel like strangers toward those with whom we ought to share the most. We have looked on, or maybe lodged a quiet protest, while with an appalling predictability the church funds are drained off into building programs or schemes for the preservation and maintenance of the church's institutional life. We have seen the sensitive and thoughtful souls silenced, ignored, or even driven away with tragic regularity. We have been baffled by the inability of our "outreach" programs to actually reach anyone except those of an almost identical social, economic, and racial background. We have so despaired of gaining meaningful theological insight in church that we have resigned ourselves to looking elsewhere. We have wondered why an intelligent and supposedly trained minister must preach to an intelligent congregation as if they were all children. We have feared that our children are receiving mere religious indoctrination and perhaps some moral training but hardly the Christian education to life that can only take place in a living community of faith.

This bitter disappointment with congregational life has robbed many Christians of the vision of the church as the gathered people of God—persons in community, together embodying the love and power of Christ. At best, church members accustom themselves to serving as objects of religious handouts and periodic pastoral care, or maybe they "get involved" and become familiar and contented figures in an efficient social/religious organization. At worst, reflective Christians are overcome with a crippling cynicism towards the organized church.

Everyone knows that the whole Christian church in our society is in a time of transition and that the shape of its future life is in question. Many Christians regard even all the confusions of such a time as a happy moment when the church may be able to clarify

and deepen its identity in Jesus Christ. But what has to be repeated again and again is that the primary level of exchange for
such deepening and clarifying is not at that level where policies
are argued, where unity schemes are debated, or where wide-scale
initiatives are "launched." The most crucial level of response is
where person meets person in the promise of Jesus, where what
is at stake is nothing less than the sufferings and joys and tasks of
this day, and where what is being renewed is nothing less than
life itself. Again, Moltmann has pointed to the possibilities.

> The crisis of the national and established churches in "Chris-
> tian" countries of long standing which has so often been de-
> scribed—the churches' loss of function, the apathy of their
> members and their slowness to move—is a chance to build up the
> fellowship church and to realize the principle of the congrega-
> tion, the community.[7]

The Lord of the church does not leave us to our own devices.
Still he visits his people as that disturbing and beckoning presence. His way of death and resurrection still stands as the paradigm for our way of thinking and imagining, as well as for our way
of doing and living. We are free to think new thoughts and search
for new ways of service in the church, to strike out on new and
uncertain journeys. Christ still appears between us on the journey. People can affect structures. Where two or three are gathered
in his name, there is still the power of his presence.

THE WORLD

There is another question to be asked, another angle of approach from which we must clarify the meaning of Christian community: the life of the church must be judged not only in relation
to the integrity of the individual Christian person but also in relation to the wider society that surrounds it. This is the question
of relevance, and it is a notoriously double-edged question. As
Dean Inge said, the church that marries the spirit of the age will

---

[7]Ibid., xvi.

be a widow in the next generation. Yet if the sufferings and aspirations of the age do not press upon the heart of the Christian community, then that community has lost its vision of the Incarnation. In Christ, the creator God was bound to the created world. In Christ, "God so loved the world." What God has joined together Christians too often wish to pull apart.

Can the local *ecclesia* be a place of intersection for the world and the love of God? Can our congregations be signs—partial and fragmentary, but also empirical and visible—of God's co-humanity with us in Christ? What meaning can the small Christian congregation have for the women and men in our urban society? Can these communities honestly commend themselves to these men and women as a truthful response to the dilemmas we all face whether we are Christians or not?

It has become commonplace to point to the fact that our common life is under threat. We mean, of course, more than the bomb. We mean all that has led to the bomb—all that tends toward our diminishing and destruction—the greed, the rootlessness, the anxiety, the injustice, the collapse of community. Burdened, but hopeful in God, we ask how we may enter the task of building a genuine human life for ourselves and others in the face of such threats. Where is the task to be engaged?

Very many women and men, very many Christians, respond to the inevitable insecurity of life by retreating into a quest for private good and fulfillment. Life is sought at the level of "me and my own." Millions of individuals and families literally live to themselves. Each one forms an independent unity—emotionally, economically, physically independent of one another. Independence is, in fact, the advertised goal of such a way of life.

Such independence is, of course, a complete illusion. It is an interesting paradox that this pursuit of individualism has something of the herd about it. We are quick to recognize this in the chains, nose rings, and green and purple hair of the "punk rockers," but we do not so easily recognize it in the herd-like materialism of the successful modern person. As Carlyle Marney said, "The individual is the self with its things. The person is the self with the selves who created and called him out."[8] Entombed in a shroud of self-concern, many people experience no living and costly connections with others or with the common good. The moment a person turns his or her heart toward God this illusion of independence begins to die.

Nevertheless, it is still true that Christianity is often co-opted to serve a false individualism. A private piety or "personal" (meaning private) communion with God, individual "spiritual" progress, "inner" peace and moral perfection—all of this can be woven into a self-centered religion with little consciousness of the communion in God with all living creatures, or indeed, with the man, woman, or child just next to us. In such a religion even love for our neighbor is urged primarily as the crowning achievement of the quest for our own perfection. In this spirit of private religious good a person may be a member of some Christian body in the same sense as he or she may be a member of any number of organizations so as to be served up with certain desirable goods and experiences. Being an organic part of the sacramental reality of the body of Christ, however, is not a concern. This is why for many Christians the word *church* conveys no compelling reality.

There are others, disillusioned with so individual a way, sensitive almost to the point of depression to the large-scale injustices and suffering in the world, for whom a deep indignation has meant a dramatic reorientation of their lives according to another principle of organization. They see that only if we band together around a clearly defined cause can such evils be confronted. For them commitment to God has come to be defined largely in terms of time and energy spent in the organized fight for the causes of world peace, world hunger, the rights of the poor and racial minorities, and the fuller freedom of women.

Some who have been drawn into such struggles have simply given up on the church altogether, and it is not difficult to see why. They cannot abide the failure to see clearly, feel deeply, and act effectively on the part of the majority of church members. Or per-

---

[8]Carlyle Marney, *Priests to Each Other* (Valley Forge PA: Judson Press, 1974) 34.

haps they hang on to the church as at least a possible avenue of propaganda for such vital aims.

It would be foolish to diminish one whit the urgency of the issues of world hunger or the threat of massive nuclear destruction. Yet it needs to be said as clearly as possible that life pursued predominantly on the collective and organizational level sooner or later becomes impersonal, passionless, and counterproductive. Even the most just of causes has a way of degenerating into an abstraction unless the concrete human connections are kept alive. Here we have in mind those who burn with anger over the injustices in the relations between the northern and southern hemispheres, yet who mysteriously never find the time and attention to share their own tables with the clearly visible persons who languish before their eyes.

We must somehow discern the paradox of a Jesus who fostered more than anyone else the dream of *shalom*, of universal justice and peace, yet who showed little interest in "mustering the troops" in the cause of the new order. There is not the slightest enthusiasm in the words of Jesus for love and justice as abstractions. He knows no course of thought which sets one class of humanity against another or which loses sight of persons in a burning concern for "the masses." If he communicated in so powerful a way the universality of the love of God, he did so because he so readily brought to bear on concrete life situations the particular demands of love. For Jesus the issues of love and justice always began just at the door, right within one's reach. In the Gospels the all-inclusive claims of love are made concrete in the face of the particular human dilemma. In the gospel vision every human being is himself or herself a universe to be revered. As Malcolm Muggeridge has remarked, the idea that the angels in heaven rejoice more over one repentant sinner than over all the righteous is not a very sound statistical proposition.

Does this mean giving up the larger perspective, the claims of the universal? Is this a call to abandon the "larger issues" of peace and justice? Obviously not. There is a desperate need to honor the broad and far-reaching claims of love, to recognize the unity of all humankind in God, to acknowledge that the hungry of Africa, the politically exploited in Latin America, and the "enemy" in the

Soviet Union are indeed our sisters and brothers before God. This
is the truth, and we cannot live justly if we cannot order our common life by this truth.

But where are men and women to touch that truth and nourish
it? "It is true that all men are brothers," wrote E. F. Schumacher,
"but it is also true that in our active personal relationships we can,
in fact, be brothers to only a few of them, and we are called to show
more brotherliness to them than we could possibly show to the
whole of mankind."[9] Is it really surprising that "slow-moving"
church members cannot lift their eyes to the plight of the poor in
far places when they find no real human communion in the very
place where love ought to flourish?

Love and justice are not learned through the repetition of
words, even less by the increase of guilt. There is, of course, nothing easier than to produce guilt in the hearts of our sisters and
brothers. But we have not found that new love and effective action happen that way.

Where then is universal love made visible and real? Perhaps
no one has addressed this question more persistently than the
Christian philosopher, Gabriel Marcel.

> We must understand that universality has its place in the dimen-
> sion of depth and not that of breadth. . . . There can be no authen-
> tic depth except where there can be real communion; but there
> will never be any real communion between individuals centered
> on themselves, and in consequence morbidly hardened, nor in the
> heart of the mass. . . . It is only within groups that are fairly re-
> stricted in size and animated by a spirit of love that the universal
> can really embody itself.[10]

The push of the universal Love to find particular expression
through in-depth communion lies at the heart of Christian vision,
which believes that the Word became flesh at a particular time and

---

[9]E. F. Schumacher, *Small Is Beautiful* (New York: Harper and Row,
1973) 65.

[10]Gabriel Marcel, *Man Against Mass Society*, trans. G. S. Fraser (South
Bend IN: Gateway Editions, 1978) 267.

place. The question of how the Christian congregation can be a concrete sign of such a love in our particular time and place lies at the heart of these reflections.

Where can the roots grow for a genuine Christian activism? In his book *Call to Conversion,* an uncompromising appeal for Christian resistance to the dominant values of our society, Jim Wallis of Sojourners has written,

> The greatest need in our time is not simply for *kerygma,* the preaching of the gospel; nor for *diakonia,* service on behalf of justice; nor for *charisma,* the experience of the Spirit's gifts; nor even for *propheteia,* the challenging of the king. The greatest need of our time is for *koinonia,* the call simply to be the church, to love one another, and to offer our lives for the sake of the world. The creation of living, breathing, loving communities of faith at the local church level is the foundation of all the other answers.[11]

This is a somewhat startling statement coming from so unrelenting an activist. It grows out of experience in the search for a faithful and honest discipleship. It is a call to deepen Christian activism at its core.

This task—what we have called the "small work" of being and building the local community—will seem to many simply too small, too tied up with the dull, average life of the dull, average church, too particular and restricted to be relevant to society's most urgent needs, too naive in the face of corporate and structural evil. But is it not really a sacrilege to speak about "the needs of our society" without speaking about the transformation of persons? The task is, in Schumacher's phrase, not human agriculture but human horticulture.

After all, is it not a complete illusion to conceive of evil as that which we can defeat by marshaling numbers and mustering influence? There is surely no more certain road to hopelessness than the facile assumption that we can save ourselves or our society by largeness, power, influence, or collective will. We will simply look

---

[11]Jim Wallis, *The Call to Conversion* (New York: Harper and Row, 1982) 109.

in vain to the secular or religious wielders of power, to the established or the radical seats of influence, for the life we need. This is the message of the cross, which put on public display all the pretensions of power and spoke with God's hidden eloquence about a new creative suffering love (Col. 2:15).

The work of Christian community calls for our energies, because here is a level of involvement that forces us to abandon our isolation for the claims of love; yet here too we are not deceived by power. For our true powerlessness, which is our way to God, is not disguised by the false claims of the collective. Where we are gathered in the name of Jesus, where person faces person in his presence, we can enter the struggles of life and embrace our brothers and sisters in the world from a station of love in humility. After all, there simply is no power over evil, no redemption at all, outside love. Not love idealized but love embodied. We have known for twenty centuries that the incarnation of love takes place only in the humble places, in the small "Bethlehems of fervor."[12] Can our congregations be such birth places of love? Can we serve the incarnation of love in the fullness of our human experience and so be a living sign of Christ in the world?

---

[12]The image comes from Gabriel Marcel, *The Decline of Wisdom*, trans. Manya Harari (London: Harvill Press, 1954) 15.

2

GATHERED
IN THE WORLD

For Christians are distinguished from the rest of humanity neither by country, language, nor customs. They do not dwell in cities of their own, nor do they use some strange language, nor practice a peculiar kind of life. . . . While dwelling in Greek or barbarian cities, as each has received his lot, and following the local customs in dress, food, and the rest of life, they display the marvellous and admittedly unusual constitution of their own citizenship. They live in their native countries, but as sojourners. They share all things, as citizens; and they endure all things as foreigners. Every foreign land is their fatherland, and every fatherland is a foreign land to them.

Epistle to Diognetus

In the world as a living sign of Christ—this possibility for the Christian congregation is filled with high hope and inescapable tension. Though gathered in the world in the name of Christ, for the sake of the world, the church is persistently tempted to escape into various forms of piety that have the paradoxical added attraction of allowing it to be comfortably and uncritically accommodated to the reigning values of contemporary culture.

In this chapter we are concerned with understanding something of the nature of the world in which the congregation is gathered. The very content of the gospel rivets the church's attention to the context of its life, for the world is the object of God's love (John 3:16). Christian congregations must live with the inherent tension implicit in Jesus' prayer that his disciples should be in the world but not of the world. How can we love the world without trusting in it, respond to the world without being conformed to it, be involved in the world without being overcome by it? Even a brief glance at the recent history of contemporary Christian congregations suggests that all too often we have reversed the order in our relationship to the world. We have trusted in the world and all that it gives to us more than we have loved it with the redemptive *agape* of Christ. We have been more conformed to its values than we have responded to its deepest areas of need. We have been overcome by its allure rather than being places for the incarnation of transforming love.

Since the Christian congregation can neither live nor love in the abstract or the ideal, but only in the local and the particular, it becomes imperative for the community of faith to understand the terrain on which it lives and carries out its mission. While there are specific realities that must be addressed by each local congregation, there are two biblical models that are helpful in describing the contours of human experience and mentality. The first of these is the question of the Psalmist: "How shall we sing the Lord's song in a foreign land?" (Ps. 137:4). The second image is what the New Testament writers called the "principalities and powers" (Gal. 4:1-11, Eph. 6:10ff, Col. 2:13-15). These images enable us to picture our world and the church's place in it in a way that is not easily understood or sufficiently explained by the use of analytical language or objective description.

THE FOREIGN LAND

The Hebrew poet who wrote Psalm 137 was among a group of displaced persons held in Babylonian captivity with no hope of a

quick return to Jerusalem. As aliens in a foreign land they wres-
tled with their relationship to the surrounding culture. As believers in an unrecognized deity they struggled to keep their faith and
to find ways of expressing it. As a despised minority subjected to
massive pressures to conform, they felt the strain of hostile propaganda and the allure of domestication. Their identity as the
people of God was constantly under threat, and there was the ever
present temptation to come to terms with their environment. In
response to the chiding of their captors, "Sing us one of the songs
of Zion," they asked, "How can we sing the Lord's song in a foreign land?" How was it possible to celebrate their faith when Yahweh was not even acknowledged in the Babylonian pantheon?
How could they speak of God's power in the humiliation of their
defeat and powerlessness?

This is an image of extraordinary illumination for Christian
congregations that seek to understand the context for faith in urban society. As in Babylon, other gods seem to be triumphant in
the city. Our goal is not to offer an analysis of contemporary society but simply to mention four realities that suggest that the
Christian congregation today is, like Israel, faced with singing
God's song in a foreign land.

Ours is a *world without Christendom*. In Western urban society there is no longer a "one-world" view based on the centrality
of the Christian church and the power of its institutions to interpret and regulate virtually every arena of life. We do not mourn
the passing of Christendom; it contained its own variety of problems for Christian life and faith and left what is in some ways a
dark legacy. Yet the Christian congregation is gathered in a world
where it cannot make assumptions about the Christian view of
reality, and it is an utter illusion to speak of a Christian society.

Accompanying the passing of Christendom was the *rise of
pluralism*. Ours is a foreign land in that the faith we hold is held
in the context of many faiths, both religious and secular. The God
we worship may not be recognized in the pantheon of gods in
contemporary culture. The radical monotheism of the Judeo-
Christian tradition must find its way once again in the midst of a
persistent practical polytheism that marks the modern mentality
and experience. While many of us may have grown up in a world

where Christian thought forms and values were normative, there are now many ways to interpret reality and to understand one's identity in it. We can no longer expect the Christian faith to be learned or experienced by osmosis. In the company of Jesus there is no place for a "forced faith." But in a pluralistic society there is every danger of a "forgotten faith."

The church is also gathered in a *secular world*. We can only rejoice in the gains of secularity over ignorance and superstition and in the fact that the church is taking responsibility for the cares and concerns of this world. The Christian is no more separated from the world than God is separated from everyday life. History is the arena of the Christian congregation's involvement. The community that attempts to withdraw from history, or deny it, looks for justification for such an attitude to a source other than the God of history. On the other hand, the Christian community must recognize that it lives in a world where life is being reduced systematically to the horizontal plane. In a "religion of secularism" any talk of God is categorized as meaningless. We have experienced the loss of transcendence, replacing it with a world of immediacy. The tragedy in the secular transition is that the declaration of human autonomy has not led to the humanization of life. The Christian congregation is gathered in a world that continues to struggle with the question of how to keep human life human. Yet where God is viewed by many as an anachronism of another age, there is a blatant refusal to acknowledge the connection between the loss of transcendence and the process of dehumanization.

Finally, just as the people of Israel had been uprooted from their homeland and scattered along the rivers of Babylon, so too is our *world marked by rootlessness*. For many the personal life story can no longer be told as a novel but only as a series of short stories. Continuity is lost in the thread of personal identity. There is no overarching theme. This has not only affected individuals, but in many cases has caused loss of community or of the significant group. Loneliness and alienation are endemic to our age. How can life be nourished at the deepest human level without roots? How can love grow without connections? With no deep reservoir of a shared past to enrich life, countless people clutch for sustenance in whatever experience will give assurance that they are not alone, that they matter, regardless of how shallow, superficial, or transient that experience may be.

These are some of the aspects of our world evoked by the imagery of the "foreign land." Here the church is called upon to sing God's song—to celebrate life, to love the world, to minister to need, to share the faith. But God is a foreigner, strangely quiet. We are exiles and sojourners and often meet one another as strangers. Our faith language is alien; our story is in danger of being forgotten; our Christian identity is being usurped by other more pressing, secular claims; our theology, long forgotten in most congregations, is losing its power to interpret and make sense out of life.

The dilemma for us is as it was for our Hebrew ancestors—resistance or capitulation. To a great extent this book is trying to suggest ways we might sing God's song in a foreign land. But such imagery does not tell the whole story about our context. Another is needed. And the New Testament language of "principalities and powers" provides it.

PRINCIPALITIES AND POWERS

To the church of his day Paul clearly sounds a Christian call to spiritual arms against the forces of evil, bondage, and death that are arrayed against human life. It is a time for battle dress and battle, not evening dress and peaceful coexistence. "For we are not contending against flesh and blood, but against the principalities, against the powers, against the world rulers of the present darkness, against the spiritual hosts of wickedness in the heavenly places. Therefore take the whole armor of God" (Eph. 6:12-13).

It is admittedly difficult for affluent North American Christians to sense the urgency of Paul's call to arms for a life and death struggle. Where life is comfortable, if not luxuriant, we are inclined toward softness. Yet even here the cracks on the surface of our lives are apparent. When life is painful we tend to grow numb. When life is confusing in its complexities we verge on paralysis. When life is broken we drift toward withdrawal, secreting a protective shell around our isolation. Countless hours of pastoral conversations have made it clear that many people, regardless of whether they are affluent or poor, experience life more as a threat than as a celebration, as something that is "happening to them" rather than as something they confidently live.

This is the kind of reality Paul is describing when he speaks of living under the domination of the principalities and powers. Elsewhere he describes it as being in slavery to the "elemental spirits" (Gal. 4:3, 8, 9; Col. 2:20). The freedom we experience in baptism is a celebration of the victory of Christ on the cross over the principalities and powers (Col. 2:12-15). The great danger exists, however, that we may still live under the dominion of the principalities and powers, as if we still belonged to them, as if we were still "of the world" (Col. 2:20). Paul's symbolic or mythological language (principalities, powers, world rulers of this present darkness, elemental spirits, thrones) is used to convey a fundamental truth about forces in this world that impinge on human life and influence structures of human society. They are fallen powers, setting themselves over against the power and purposes of God, following the god of this age (2 Cor. 4:4). Where once they were meant to enhance, order, and serve human life, in their fallenness they tend to corrupt, blind, and enslave human life. They demand loyalty and allegiance.[1]

Paul's experience of the threat of the principalities and powers to life and freedom in the first century is only confirmed by our experience in the twentieth. Sociology has long pointed out that institutions, economic structures, bureaucracies, nationalisms, ideologies, and religions are more than the sum of the individuals who make them up or participate in them. They seem to have a life of their own; no single individual or group really has control over them. They certainly have the power to name, set standards of orthodoxy, accuse, condemn, and reward. The power of the powers can be felt in the very texture of life, for they work at a structural level in all aspects of a society—intellectual struc-

---

[1]See Jim Wallis, *Agenda for Biblical People* (New York: Harper and Row, 1976) chapter three, for an excellent discussion of "principalities and powers."

tures (ologies and isms), moral structures, religious structures, political structures, and economic structures.

Let us give a few examples.

- The Christian must be aware that the *state* can demand an allegiance that intrudes upon the loyalty claimed by Christ. We must learn to live under the state, and the collective exercise of its power and enticement, without surrendering an obedience that belongs only to Christ.
- The principalities and powers function in a forceful way to set person against person through the dynamics of *class consciousness* and *racial prejudice*.
- They are at work in the whole area of *economics* as human life becomes ordered solely around financial issues until we become "owned" by what we own.
- *Public opinion* can assert such an influence on our lives that we can scarcely claim to act on the basis of free choice and conscience.
- *Corporations* can hold such sovereign sway over their employees that "work" can become a form of alienation from life and "security" a form of servitude. A chain is a chain whether made of gold or iron!

In addition to the power of each of these individual entities, there is the fact that they interlock with each other. The result is a synergistic force and power that seems to move beyond our ability to influence. Celebration, freedom, and dignity can be sapped away from human life.

Every person lives with, in, and through all of these realities. The issue for the Christian is not whether the "powers" and their manifestation in the structures of life can be avoided but whether or not they are allowed to become ultimate. The deceptive illusion created by the principalities and powers in any of these areas is that these various structures really do define reality, that they are of ultimate value, that one had better play the game according to their rules, and that they are at the center of history and importance. All reality is defined by reference to them and their own self-interest. Allegiance forms the identity of those who participate. It is no wonder that many people experience life with a growing sense of powerlessness. The structures in which we live seem to dictate our patterns of life.

If we are blinded by the weapons of illusion and allow our hearts and minds to be seduced by the propaganda of the principalities and powers, if we concede the ultimacy of any of these structures, we will simply bow down in idolatry. If we cannot break the tyranny of the principalities and powers as they dominate our lives through the dictates of the structures, we will simply bow down in oppression. The claim of the Christian gospel, on the other hand, is liberation from the principalities and powers through the victory of Jesus Christ. It is clear that for Paul, especially in Galatians, Romans, Ephesians, and Colossians, salvation is not only from personal sin, but is liberation from slavery to the powers.

It is not too much to say that the Christian congregation is gathered in a world that is a battleground where the fallen powers seek to dominate and enslave human life while Christ seeks to free it. The powers are at work wherever there is a systematic diminishing of our humanity. Their weapons, so ingeniously unleashed in the structures of society, are seduction, lies, propaganda, violence (overt or hidden), fear, and bewitchment by technical manipulation (whether that technical manipulation be scientific, economic, psychological, or religious). Property is valued over people, and personhood is lost in the mindless management of the masses. The individual is reduced to the status of "thing." The powers entice us at every level of our identity where the question "Who am I?" is actually lived. Because the principalities and powers dominate the structures of contemporary life, that question is customarily answered in terms of one's work, race, nationality, politics, money, social standing, or family.

In the midst of such domination the Christian congregation is called to ask, "Who or what do you call Lord?" It raises this question because it recalls the most searching question of all put by him whom it confesses as Lord: "What shall a person give in exchange for his or her life?" Where and how have we sold our souls into slavery? To the corporation? To the state? To greed? To security? To status?

Is there any place a person can stand to face the power of the powers? The Christian congregation, the human church, can witness to the victory of Christ over the principalities and powers by creating zones of liberation and resistance in the world. It remains for us to picture as clearly as possible how the congregation in the modern world can act in community to name the powers and to deny their ultimacy in determining life. But if, as we have argued, the powers are at work wherever there is a systematic diminishing of our humanity, then surely this process must begin with the reaffirmation of our humanity in the vision of the true human being—Jesus Christ.

3

A HUMAN GATHERING

He also, in the end of times, for the recapitulation of all things, is become a man among people, visible and tangible, in order to abolish death and bring to light life, and bring about the communion of God and humanity. And the third article is the Holy Spirit . . . who . . . has been poured forth in a new manner upon humanity over all the earth renewing people to God.

Irenaeus

*T*he earliest Christian writings make a strange and wonderful claim: Jesus Christ is the new human being, and the gathering of men and women around him signifies the coming of a new humanity. The people of Jesus point to a new creation in which all of life is granted a new dignity in the redeeming work of God. For Christians this new humanity is an accomplished fact in Jesus Christ. But it is also an aspiration by which the Christian church lives. Being newly human is a work that Christians have been given to do.

These days the phrase "new humanity" speaks with a new eloquence, since it has become clear that living a genuinely human life is never an assumption but a challenge. For "humanity" means far more than a biological species. It means also a distinctive quality of life, a dimension of love, awareness, and responsibility that reaches far deeper than simple existence. The old excuse, "after all, we are only human," cannot do justice to our situation. Indeed, living well and responsibly means exactly being "only human," that is, being not less than human.

The Christian congregation ought to be a cradle and a home for the human, a place where our distinctively human capacities can be nourished and guarded and strained after. Being a Christian ought to make a person more, not less, human.

To ask "What does it mean to be better human beings?" is to raise the problem of values and norms. One of the paradoxes of our society is that it stands or falls with certain beliefs about the dignity of human beings. But these norms also carry within themselves the possibility of their own destruction. We espouse freedom and tolerance, which means that no given meaning, value, or model should be dictated or forced upon us. Such freedom and tolerance reveal a healthy suspicion of power and are meant to keep one group from dominating another. They are intended to guard human dignity. But it is obvious that freedom and tolerance are not ends. They can only provide the conditions under which we must choose and pursue the life we believe to be truly human. Very many men and women have suffered a disorientation about what it means to live a "good" or a "fulfilled" human life.

JESUS CHRIST THE TRUE HUMAN BEING

For Christians Jesus Christ is the measure of the truly human life. But just at this point the church has often stumbled, because we have failed to uphold the ancient Christian faith in the real humanity of our Lord.

Outside the church, Jesus may be regarded as an important "past master," but no one really believes he is God. That is no surprise; it is just what one would expect to find. What is not so obvious is that inside the church many Christians do not believe in the *humanity* of Jesus. These two forms of unbelief are not so far apart as they at first seem. If only the church believed more in the humanity of Jesus, we would make a far more convincing witness in the world to his divinity.

In order to more clearly understand this dilemma, we must take a brief detour into the roads of Christian history and theology. In fact, our theological detour will turn out to be the main highway to everything else we want to say about the Christian congregation. In the earliest Christian centuries the church suffered under persecution from without. But *from within*, the first great threat to the faith was a denial of the full humanity of Jesus. For many Christians, especially those steeped in hellenistic thought, a "human god" was an intolerable idea, since "flesh," the body, all the material creation, was viewed with a deep pessimism. Flesh could not bear spirit. The flesh was either a neutral temporary husk to be cast off by spirit, or it was positively evil. Between God and the material creation there could be no real converse. This division was so extreme that some of these "gnostics" posited a lesser god or "demiurge" as creator of the world, and a higher god who was the remote supreme divinity.

From the perspective of such an extreme dualism between flesh and spirit, the real humanity of God in Jesus Christ was an abhorrent doctrine. These "docetists" (from *dokein*, "to seem") held that Jesus clearly *seemed* to be a human being, but actually was not. Docetism in the early church was a tendency, not a formulated and unified doctrine. There is ample evidence that a similar tendency toward a deep-seated pessimism about the flesh persists in the church and that subtle forms of docetism weave their way into our belief. It is easy to see how Christians, anxious for the uniqueness and divinity of Jesus in an unbelieving world, could embrace an "accelerated super-naturalism," forgetting that what is unique to Christianity is not belief in God, but belief in *God in the flesh.*

Against a persistent leaning toward docetism in Christian piety, the New Testament and the traditional teaching of the church speak for a wholly human Jesus. When John wrote, "concerning the word of life . . . that which we have seen with our eyes, which we have looked upon and touched with our hands" (1 John

1:1), he was contending for the full weight of the Incarnation. Three hundred fifty years later, at the Council of Chalcedon (A.D. 451), the church's faith in the Incarnation was expressed in these words:

> Following the holy fathers, we all unanimously teach . . . one and the same Son, our Lord Jesus Christ, the same perfect in Godhead and the same perfect in manhood, truly God and truly man, the same of a rational soul and body.[1]

This confession pushes both the divinity and the humanity of Jesus to the limits. He is "fully God," not simply a superior prophet or even a heavenly being. And this same Jesus did not merely appear or pretend to be a human being; he was "fully man." Jesus who is God is genuinely human. And this genuinely human Jesus is God—*Emmanuel,* God with us—sharing our common humanity. The Chalcedonian council went on to confess that this union of God and humanity did not mean that Jesus was "half God and half human." Rather, he was "one and the same Christ . . . made known in two natures without confusion, without change, without division, without separation."[2] Christ is no piece of divine patchwork, God and humanity somehow welded together. His two "natures" are woven in a seamless garment called Incarnation.

Two points are important for clarification. This Chalcedonian statement is not *explanation;* it is *confession*—a confession of the mystery that Christians have been pondering for twenty centuries. No one with any sense has ever claimed this is simple. After all, God and God's actions are bound to be larger than our rationality. You cannot pour a universe of truth into the limited containers of even the deepest human minds. The "Chalcedonian formula" simply sets the boundaries, "fully God" and "fully human," within which we can explore the mystery of Christ.

---

[1]*Acta conciliorum oecumenicorum,* ed. E. Schwartz, translated and quoted in J. N. D. Kelly, *Early Christian Doctrines* (New York: Harper and Row, 1960) 339.

[2]Ibid.

Secondly, this mystery of a fully human, fully divine Jesus was not simply "made up" by the theologians in an attempt to give Christian faith maximum honor and authority. Rather, the doctrine about the Incarnation is the attempt to cling tenaciously to the *experienced mystery* of Christ. The earliest disciples knew Jesus as a man. He ate, drank, slept, wept, taught, laughed, and suffered with them as a man. But in his fully human company they began to experience a new world, a new dimension transcending the human and the temporal. In his presence the word "God" was transformed into the most immediate and winsome of realities. This new presence was so strong, this life so utterly graceful, that they began to call this man by the ancient titles of divine honor: "Son of God," "Christ." The scandalous death of Jesus crushed and silenced these claims, but only for a moment. These same disciples met this Jesus in his resurrection, in his new humanity. Again he ate with them and taught them and graced them with an utterly new passion for life, an eternal life. This new meeting was so solid, so sure, so shared, so convincing, that these disciples never stopped speaking and acting in the name of this Jesus, even in the face of their own deaths.

Briefly stated, that is the experienced mystery that stands behind the Christian doctrine of the Incarnation. The thrust of this mystery is summarized clearly by C. F. D. Moule.

> A person who had recently been crucified, but is found to be alive, with "absolute" life, the life of the age to come, and is found, moreover, to be an inclusive, all embracing presence—such a person is beginning to be described in terms appropriate to nothing less than God himself.[3]

That Jesus was God, without ceasing to be a human person, is the mystery out of which grows the fully human yet divinely moved life of the Christian.

There are three points especially at which many Christians, in wanting to give Jesus the honor due to him, end in a subtle denial

---

[3]C. F. D. Moule, *The Origin of Christology* (Cambridge: Cambridge University Press, 1977) 53.

of his full humanity. The sad result is that Jesus is finally blocked off from our common human plight.

Miracles. Fewer and fewer scholars deny that Jesus was a miracle-worker. The evidence is all for it, and there is less arrogant assurance than there used to be about what "just does not happen" in the world. But believers often miss the meaning of Jesus' miracles by seeing them as sheerly supernatural portents done because a divine Christ can do anything. The miracles therefore class Jesus way above our humanity. A being who can "do anything he wants to" is not a human being at all.

In the Gospels, however, the miracles are not simply divine works; they are human works done by the power of God in faith. Jesus himself does not attribute the mighty works to any automatic power of his own. More than once Jesus says frankly, "your faith has cured you." And he assures his followers that such "signs" as he does will "follow those that believe" (Mark 16:17). The miracles are the works of humanity consecrated and submitted to God. So once when the disciples were faced with an especially intransigent demon and complained to Jesus that they could not cast him out, Jesus' answer is shocking in its appeal to human faith: "Because of your little faith you could not" (Matt. 17:20). The miracles of Jesus do not show us a superman; they reveal the Son of man, fully submitted to, and so mightily empowered by, God.

Sinlessness. The stark claim of the New Testament is that Jesus lived without sin. The response of piety to this claim is often: "well, of course, he was the Son of God! He could not sin!" But to ascribe a simple, effortless, "automatic" perfection to Jesus is to ignore the other scriptural claim, that Jesus was "tempted in all ways as we are."

The temptation scenes in the fourth chapters of Matthew and Luke are too often passed over as mere charades construed for our edification. Yet they picture Jesus in a life and death struggle with evil. In fact, here Jesus must fight for faithfulness to his mission against all the false alternatives offered by Satan ("If you are the Son of God . . ."). Jesus holds to the way of suffering and submission against Satan's offer of supernatural power. It is a struggle that continues throughout Jesus' ministry, even into the Garden of Gethsemane.

How does Jesus accomplish victory over this real temptation? The Gospels sketch a clear picture: through the *human work* of fasting, frequent prayer, and much suffering. Jesus fights and wins a genuine victory over evil. Yet he does not even own his victory: "Why do you ask me about what is good? One there is who is good" (Matt. 19:17).

Knowledge. The Gospels present Jesus as a man of extraordinary insight. He sees into the lives of others with uncanny accuracy; he knows the hearts and minds of others; he predicts his own death. From these facts Christian piety has sometimes gone on to speak of an omniscient Jesus who knows everything simply by virtue of his divinity. But "an omniscient being who knows all the answers before he thinks and all the future before he acts is not a man at all, he has escaped the human predicament."[4]

Against this picture of an omniscient mind housed in a human body, the Gospels present a man whose mind and perception grow with age, experience, confrontation, and in conformity with the Scriptures. Even in the very difficult question of Jesus' "self-consciousness" (how and when did Jesus come to an awareness of his own unique identity and mission?) the picture is one of growth and emerging clarity. In his baptism Jesus hears the heavenly voice which itself speaks in the words of the Old Testament Scriptures (Matt. 3:17; Ps. 2:7; Isa. 42:1). Through temptation and a mind soaked in the Old Testament, Jesus clarifies his own mission. It is a process that does not end even at the cross, where we hear a broken man cry, "My God, why have you forsaken me?" These words reveal the extraordinary cost of the human faithfulness of Jesus Christ. It was a faithfulness fought for with genuine human anguish. This faithfulness is the source of his unique power, goodness, and insight. His last words, if we will ponder them, are the full measure of the full humanity of Jesus Christ.

---

[4]Austin Farrer, *Interpretation and Belief* (London: SPCK, 1976) 135.

THE HUMANITY OF GOD

If it is true that God became a human being in Jesus, and yet did not cease to be God, then God has taken our humanity "into" the divine life. In a free decision of sovereign love the creator is bound to the creature. In Jesus God steps forward as our human partner. This belief brings an inexhaustible dynamic to the way Christians speak and think about God. For, as Karl Barth wrote, "It is precisely God's *deity* which, rightly understood, includes his *humanity*."[5] In Jesus Christ we look upon "the human face of God."

The Gospels are eager to communicate this truth to us by insisting on the humanity of the resurrected Christ.

> Jesus himself stood among them. But they were startled and *supposed they saw a spirit.* And he said to them, "Why are you troubled, and why do questions rise in your hearts? *See my hands and my feet, that it is I myself; handle me and see; for a spirit has not flesh and bones as you see that I have.* And while they still disbelieved for joy, and wondered, he said to them, "Have you anything here to eat?" They gave him a piece of broiled fish, *and he took it and ate before them* (Luke 24:36-43, emphasis ours).

The risen Christ offers two signs of his human identity. First, he offers the sign of his wounds. How strange that the risen Christ still bears the marks of his sufferings! He has not left his humanity behind; even the sufferings of his humanity he takes with him to God. Secondly, the risen Jesus eats "before them." Why is it that in the resurrection accounts Christ comes eating and drinking? It is his gesture of solidarity with his human companions. Before his death Jesus had been known as one who ate and drank with the sinners. Almost his last act with his disciples was a shared meal. Now, in his risen new humanity, the Christ comes again eating and drinking with those who had forsaken him at his cross, restoring his human fellowship with them. For the Jews, indeed for all peo-

---

[5]Karl Barth, *The Humanity of God* (Richmond: John Knox Press, 1960) 16.

ple, the shared meal is the most excellent sign and celebration of our human solidarity. In interpreting the story of Abraham's hosting of the angels in Genesis 18, the Rabbi Zusya commented that through Abraham the angels were allowed to join in the distinctively human privilege—the sharing of food before God.[6]

In his resurrected and ascended humanity (what the theologians have called his perpetual humanity) Jesus Christ bears our humanity in its sufferings and celebrations into the very life of God. "There is one mediator between God and men, *the man Christ Jesus*" (1 Tim. 2:5). We must always remind ourselves of this truth; we must never forget that to love and serve God, to be the partners of God, we are not called upon to be other than human beings. God meets us, lives with us and in us, here in our human lives. This humanity, which we too often treat as a slum dwelling, is God's temple.

THE HUMANITY OF THE PEOPLE OF GOD

The subtle docetism, the tendency to minimize the humanity of Jesus, goes hand in hand with a subtle denial of our own humanity. Has not the church often seemed fearful and suspicious of its own humanity? Are the critics right, that no matter what theories about a new humanity Christians want to spin out, the fact is that the Christian stance makes people anti-human, afraid to be human, and so, less than human?

In fact, on this point as on many others, the church's critics have been both right and wrong. From our own experience in Christian congregations, each of us has touched and been touched by a breadth and depth of humanity we may not have found elsewhere. We are nourished by the friendships, still breathing across too much time and space, held intact by the spirit of love we shared in some gathering of Christians. Many of us can record those stretching encounters with persons of very different race, different ages, different educational backgrounds—encounters that may never have happened outside our participation in the life of some

---

[6]Quoted by Martin Buber in *The Way of Man* (Secaucus NJ: Citadel Press, 1966) 20.

church. For many people the congregation is a place where learning continues, where they are called upon to attend seriously to
human history and human literature and to reflect critically on the
ethical and moral dimensions of life. All this is true and ought not
to be forgotten in any criticism of congregational life.

But we have known the other side as well. We have seen the
human friendship within the congregation close itself into a tight,
impenetrable ring, excluding all others who live or think differently. We have seen ethical reflection turn sour against human life
in a negation of human pleasure, joy, and natural good. We have
watched compassion wither until religion grows cold and frozen
in a lifeless ritual and nothing else. We have heard Christian leaders setting themselves against new learning, new justice, even
genuine renewal within the church; at the same time, they have
made easy accommodation with power, wealth, and the spirit of
self-preservation.

If we are ever to see deeply into our failures, we will have to
look beyond the old "conservative" versus "liberal" split in our
religious life that still racks the church, especially in the United
States. There is a conformism of the left as well as a conformism
of the right, and both are a mere accommodation to trends. The
conservatives are not conservative enough, cut off as they are from
the ancient traditions of intellect and spirituality. The liberals are
not liberal enough to move beyond theory and the patronage of just
causes from afar. The issues that divide conservatives and liberals
are not, in fact, theological enough, because they leave aside the
call to remake our lives here and now in the image of the genuinely human God.

We have said that if we believed more in the humanity of Jesus
Christ we would make better witnesses in the world to his Lordship. Perhaps now we are at the place to see how this is true. The
first disciples of Jesus came to faith in the encounter with the
unique celebrating and suffering humanity of Jesus Christ. It can
be no different for men and women today. The word we bring the
world is not a "word" in the usual sense. It cannot remain only a
principle, an idea, even a model. The word the church utters is
tied forever to what the church is, to what it is called to be—a
gathered humanity, a new co-humanity in Jesus Christ.

To believe in the humanity of God in Jesus Christ is never to despair of this human life and never to despair of this human church, what Karl Barth called the "strange communion of the strange saints." After all, where does the existence of this particular human community take its start except in the human life of God in the world? In his old age, Karl Barth wrote some words that express the conviction that moves us to write these pages.

> We believe the Church as the place where . . . humanity—the humanity of God—wills to assume tangible form in time and here upon earth. Here we recognize the humanity of God. Here we delight in it. Here we celebrate and witness to it.[7]

A NEW LOVE FOR THE WORLD

To speak of the church as a place of new humanity does not mean moral superiority. It does not mean withdrawing from others who are regarded as the "old humanity." Christian morality ought to be a high morality. But there are several roads to morality, and never has the church managed to be genuinely "better" than the others, try as it may. If "new humanity" becomes a phrase to fence off yet another human division, it becomes a tool of alienation, resentment, and hostility, and it ought never to be used at all.

The strange holiness of Jesus expressed itself in a new openness towards all the others, even those who were not holy. Jesus had all the marks of the holy man: prayer, poverty, and purity. He was one of the separate ones. Yet those who encountered him found him to be strangely near to them in their sufferings and sins.

The holiness of Christian people, our usefulness to God, will be found in a new openness to the world, a new solidarity and friendship in the world and with the world. New humanity means being newly committed to humanity, newly aligned in favor of others, newly invigorated with the passion for living the human life, newly delighted with every attempt to realize a genuinely

---

[7]Barth, *Humanity of God*, 65.

human life. A radical love for the world lies at the heart of our Christian vision: "For God so loved the world that he gave his only son" (John 3:16).

But was there not also from the beginning a realization that being a Christian means doing battle with the world? ("Do not love the world or the things of the world. If anyone loves the world, love for the Father is not in him" [1 John 2:15].) How are we to understand this love of God *for* the world and this love of God that *rejects* the world?

We believe there is no more crucial question than this for our present situation, and no one has addressed it more clearly than the monk Thomas Merton. In a chapter entitled, "Everything that is, is Holy," he writes:

> Detachment from things does not mean setting up a contradiction between "things" and "God" as if God were another thing and as if His creatures were His rivals. We do not detach ourselves from things in order to attach ourselves to God, but rather we become detached *from ourselves* in order to see and use all things in and for God. This is an entirely new perspective which many sincerely moral and ascetic minds fail utterly to see. There is no evil in anything created by God, nor can anything of His become an obstacle to our union with Him.[8]

In a genuine Christian "detachment" from the world, the dualism and the "hostility" is not between God and the world but between a false and a true self.

> The obstacle is in our "self," that is to say in the tenacious need to maintain our separate, external, egotistic will. It is when we refer all things to this outward and false "self" that we alienate ourselves from reality and from God. It is then the false self that is our god, and we love everything for the sake of this self. We use all things, so to speak, for the worship of this idol which is our imaginary self. In so doing we pervert and corrupt things, or rather we turn our relationship to them into a corrupt and sinful rela-

---

[8]Thomas Merton, *New Seeds of Contemplation* (London: Burns & Oates, 1962) 17.

tionship. We do not thereby make them evil, but we use them to increase our attachment to our illusory self.[9]

The fast and the feast are both a part of the Christian way; they stand as symbols of the apparent contradiction between a love for and a detachment from the world. Fasting is an expression of denial and renunciation. In this way of renunciation the believer "despises" the nourishment of the world in order to hold fast to the meat and drink that only God can give. For the time of the fast, flesh and spirit are set at odds, God and the world are momentarily torn asunder so that in this act of "violence" the believer may learn to choose God over the world.

But the fast ends. When Christians turn to face Christ in the most characteristic act of fellowship, then they do not come fasting, but feasting on the bread and wine, the very stuff of the earth. The Eucharist is communion with God in the world, with others, and through the simple material elements of the world. The Eucharist is the clearest affirmation of the church's solidarity with the rest of creation. It is the wedding of the simple "earthy" elements and the simple earthly, human actions with the living Christ. In this sense, the Eucharist is the sign of the real destiny of our human existence. As Buber has said, "nature needs man for what no angels can perform on it, namely, its hallowing."[10]

The fast followed by the feast is a parable of Christian life. We "hate" the world and detach ourselves from it—its fame, power, wealth, and values—as an expression of holy freedom from the world. But all of this is done to enable us to return again to the world with a new love for the world, to find a new solidarity with and enjoyment of all God's creation.

At the original creation of the world God sang again and again, "It is good." In the birth of a new creation, the angels sang, "Peace on earth, good will towards men." And when Jesus prayed he said, "Thy will be done on earth." The Christian knows this world as

---

[9]Ibid.

[10]Buber, *Way of Man*, 20.

God's doing, as God's abode, as destined for re-creating in God's will.

What does solidarity with the world mean for Christian life and mission? Here we can only point to some basic dispositions—a basic orientation that we hope will become more vivid later on. Love for the world begins with *a hospitable heart toward all the others*, even those who are very different from ourselves. The oddest, most miserable, least desirable person, the most spiritually broken—in all these we are meant to see the ones to whom Jesus Christ is brother. We are called to pierce through all that separates us in a search for that common human bond. All of us are afraid of people who act and think very differently from ourselves. Sometimes we are actually repulsed by the ugliness and desperation of others. Yet if the Christian fellowship becomes merely one division in an already divided world, it has lost touch with the very source of its life. Christian fellowship ought to mean the planting of a new inclusive love in the middle of a world torn apart by a thousand partisan, partial loves.

This longing toward others includes a deep respect for their striving toward worthwhile living. In family life, economic life, relations between women and men, education, business—wherever men and women are trying in their own ways to build a life that is decent, lasting, and human, Christians can find friendship and common cause. The others may not consciously conceive of their lives in the service of God. Yet they are answering "yes" to God's gift of life. Christians can in good conscience meet all such struggles not with proud abstention or by trying to force others prematurely into the Christian mold, but with reverence, gratitude, and participation.

Christian solidarity with the world also means *caring for others in the mystery of their wholeness*. Christian love refuses the persistent alienation of flesh from spirit, mind from emotions, religious from secular. When I move across the room to gather my child in my arms, I do not embrace only her body, or only her soul, or any abstraction called "spirit." It is *her*, in all her complex of needs and hopes and desires, whom I love—this human soul who is body and spirit. From Paul onwards Christianity has held to the belief in the resurrection of the body, because it knows that persons are whole and are meant to be redeemed in their wholeness. You can wound a person's spirit by neglecting or tormenting the body; you can kill a person by breaking the spirit. A faith that affirms the enfleshment of God cannot but hold to the mystery of human persons as bodies who are spirits and living spirits who are bodies.

Finally, Christian love for the world means *the deepest commitment to the world's destiny.* It refuses preoccupation with "personal" salvation, if that really means private salvation while "the rest of the world goes to hell." The Jewish philosopher Martin Buber has written some words that we can read only with great sadness.

> One of the main points in which Christianity differs from Judaism is that it makes each man's salvation his highest aim. Judaism regards each man's soul as a serving member of God's creation which, by man's work, is to become the Kingdom of God; thus no soul has its object in itself, in its own salvation. True, each is to know itself, purify itself, perfect itself, but not for its own sake— neither for the sake of its temporal happiness nor for that of its eternal bliss—but for the sake of the work which it is destined to perform upon the world.[11]

Is it true that Christianity makes each one's own soul his or her highest good? Is Christianity really an elevated spiritual self-centeredness? Certainly Christians have often lived as if that were true. And we cannot avoid the indictment inherent in Buber's words. However, you simply cannot go to the sources of Christianity and hold that "each one's soul is his highest aim." It was Paul, the Jewish Christian Apostle, who wrote, "I could wish that I myself were accursed and cut off from Christ for the sake of my brethren, my kinsmen by race" (Rom. 9:3). This is a radically selfless statement made out of a radical universal Christian hope.

It is true that Jesus asked, "what shall it get you if you gain the whole world and lose your own soul?" But what is that soul's highest good? "You shall love the Lord your God . . . and you shall

---

[11]Ibid., 33-34.

love your neighbor as yourself" (Luke 10:25-28). This is the answer of the Jew Jesus, who in this matter speaks for every Jew and every Christian. "Salvation" in the Christian sense means, from first to last, koinonia—participation, first in the love and glory of God, and secondly, in the good of others.

Even the Christian belief in the resurrection from the dead is not first a matter of personal survival. It is a hope of participation in the glory of God. The Christian lives for that eschatological moment in the "end," when "God will be everything to everyone" (1 Cor. 15:28). This anticipation and hope for God's glory embraces the whole of God's creation. "For the creation waits with eager longing for the revealing of the children of God . . . because the creation itself will be set free from its bondage to decay and obtain the glorious liberty of the children of God" (Rom. 8:19, 21). This cosmic hope explains why the images of "heaven" in the Christian Scriptures are not in fact ethereal, pale, or individualistic, but are as solid as the earth: a new heaven and earth, a banquet, a city, a mighty chorus.

Every Christian ought to be taught that one's own soul, one's own life, is indeed a universe in the eyes of God, destined for eternal life in God. But if each soul is a universe, each one cannot find true life without opening up to the universes that God has made. Each voice is made for a singular beauty, but it must seek to find and blend with the other voices if it is to sing a song to God. This koinonia—this chorus, this interpenetration of universes, this new creation, is the meaning of salvation.

A NEW TOGETHERNESS

The new humanity must mean a new co-humanity. One cannot speak of being made new in Christ without seeking and experiencing a new nearness to others. We say "seeking" because this new nearness is never simply a fact by virtue of our calling ourselves Christians. It is rather a promise to claim, a hope in which to live, a grace to signify. And it can be claimed, lived, and signified only by coming closer together in Christ. The new humanity is a new way of being together in the world. But what does this new togetherness mean? What prevents it being simply a lofty but empty ideal? What shape will it take in the world?

A new koinonia in material goods. We begin here because here our resistances are raised high. The very first Christian congregation was described in these terms: "And all who believed were together and had all things in common; and they sold their possessions and goods and distributed them to all, as any had need" (Acts 2:44, 45). This fact is given a surprising prominence in the early chapters of Acts, no doubt because such actions were as unusual then as they are now. Men and women do not give up possessions easily! Too often this early "communism" is explained as a historical curiosity that was a by-product of the early Christian belief that the world was about to end. But a vivid sense of the end does not of itself make people less selfish. The text itself links this new sharing with something far deeper: "those who believed were of one heart and soul . . . and great grace was upon them all (Acts 4:32, 33). Grace became flesh in the simple but radical act of giving up and giving away possessions.

It was a gesture that carried within itself its own interpretation. When Paul was fighting tooth and nail for the unity of the Gentile and Jewish churches, his primary weapon was the collection of money that he organized among the Gentile churches on behalf of the poverty-stricken Christians in Jerusalem. Paul took enormous pains with this as an unmistakable symbol of solidarity in a biracial church. This collection, and other occasions of the sharing of goods, was called, quite intentionally, the *koinonia.*[12]

We are not appealing for a simple "communism" in mere mimicry of the primitive church. But we wonder if any really new *koinonia* can take shape if we are not somehow enabled to loosen the tight grip we keep on what we regard as ours. If we are poor, such sharing sounds the note of good news. If we have much, it will take faith and the spirit of risk to allow us to see the great grace hidden beneath the renunciation. There is no automatic good in poverty. But there is a captivating eloquence in the refusal to par-

---

[12]2 Cor. 8:4; 9:13; Rom. 12:13; 15:26; Phil. 4:15; 1 Tim. 6:18.

ticipate in society's cult of abundance in order to discover a new nearness to others.

A new bearing of sins, a koinonia in forgiveness. The reality of God's forgiveness and acceptance is the life's breath of the Christian church. But how does such forgiveness become concrete except in the mutual forgiveness of a shared life?

There is in the words of Jesus a persistent vital link between the forgiveness we get and the forgiveness we give: "For if you forgive men their trespasses, your heavenly father also will forgive you; but if you do not forgive men their trespasses, neither will your father forgive your trespasses" (Matt. 6:14). This is not as simple as it looks. The link between forgiving and being forgiven is not simply a legal agreement ("I'll forgive you," says God, "if you forgive others"). The connection goes deeper. The fact is that the grace that allows us to forgive and the grace that allows us to accept God's forgiveness is one and the same grace. To breathe the air of God's forgiveness is necessarily to learn to forgive; and to genuinely seek to forgive another is to be brought near to the forgiveness of God.

The world is a place of hostility, of conflict, of ruthless competition. To live in the world is to be wronged and abused by others. More tragically, to live in the world means to wrong and abuse others. None of us escapes this web of hostility, even when our intentions are pure (and how often are our intentions entirely free of malice?). In the Christian understanding of life together, this hostility is undercut not by denial, cover-up, or polite tolerance, but by open acknowledgment, confession, and mutual forgiveness. If even small communities of men and women strive toward such forgiveness, the cycle of recrimination and competition is broken, and a new humanity begins to take shape.

The stark call of Jesus to forgive as we have been forgiven ought to help ward off any naive disillusionment in the church. Jesus warns us from the first moment we enter the Christian community that we cannot abide there without the daily giving and receiving in the *koinonia* of forgiveness.

A new koinonia in suffering. When the writer of the Epistle to the Hebrews said that the "pioneer" of our salvation was made "perfect through suffering," he meant that Jesus was made perfect in his solidarity with his human brothers and sisters. "For he who sanctifies and those who are sanctified have all one origin. That is why he is not ashamed to call them brethren" (Heb. 2:10, 11). In his cross Christ's humanity is welded to ours. The humanity of God reaches so far as to suffer with "the least" of the human family (Matt. 25:40). This is why it is not too much to say that the reality of a new humanity stands or falls here. Can our Christian congregations be made "perfect" through suffering? That is, can we share our sufferings, welcome others who suffer, and so discover a new solidarity under the cross?

It is wishful thinking to speak simply of relieving or "eradicating" the suffering around us, though we must do the best we can. But our distinctive call is to hold to those who suffer in the poverty of faith, to "weep with those who weep" in the transforming love of the cross. This mission calls with a special urgency today. Such fellowship in sufferings is no "solution" to the "problem" of suffering. Yet it has the power to root out apathy and despair and bring a new passion and reverence to life. And there lives within such a fellowship the possibility of the reconciliation between the moment of suffering and the moment of joy.

A new koinonia in joy. If even our suffering and our sins cannot drive us apart; if our sins bring occasion for forgiveness and our sufferings deepen our love for one another, what can keep us from celebration and enjoyment of one another? Paul wrote, "Rejoice always" (Phil. 4:4) and "give thanks in all circumstances" (1 Thess. 5:18). How strange such words sound next to our conditioned and fragile bids for happiness! How often the Christian church has gone about its business absent of any discernible joy! Even Christians look everywhere except to the church for their happiness. Surely the New Testament makes clear that "Where Jesus is, there is life. There is abundant life, vigorous life, loved life, and eternal life. There is life-before-death."[13] Nothing betrays a false Christianity faster than an affected, strained "joy," a joy that betrays its insecurity by ceaseless chatter about "how

---

[13]Jürgen Moltmann, *The Open Church*, trans. M. D. Meeks (London: SCM Press, 1978) 19.

wonderful it is to be a Christian." But nothing communicates the mysterious presence of Christ more readily than that deep-flowing, abiding joy that is woven throughout even our sorrows. Such a joy is not ours to create. Nor is it to be sought for its own sake. It is the gift we receive from Christ as we bind our humanity to his in *koinonia* with our brothers and sisters.

PART II

THERE AM I IN THE MIDST OF THEM

4

A PLACE
OF PASTORAL CARE

We pray you, Master, be our helper and protector. Save those of us in affliction, have mercy on the humble, raise up the fallen, manifest yourself to those in need, heal the sick, bring back those of your people who are straying. Feed the hungry, ransom our prisoners, raise up the weak, comfort the faint-hearted. Let all the nations know you that you are God alone and Jesus Christ is your servant and we are your people and the sheep of your pasture.

Clement of Rome

In the primal story of the dissolution of human community through the power and effect of sin, two realities are prefigured that have become part and parcel of our experience. The first is the human attempt to hide our nakedness from God. The second is the desire to evade responsibility for our fellow creatures. In both cases our primal selves are exiled to the land of Nod, east of Eden. Nod, the "place of wandering," symbolizes the loneliness of alienation from ourselves and our brothers and sisters. The first reality is depicted in the story of Adam and Eve, who, having eaten of the forbidden fruit, hide themselves from the presence of the Lord in the foliage of the garden. God seeks them out with the question, "Where are you?" The second reality is depicted in the story of Cain, who, having slain his brother Abel, is also sought by God. Now the question is, "Where is your brother?"

Where are you? Where is your brother (sister)? These two questions coupled with the other interrogatives—who and why— form the twin foci of pastoral concern within the Christian congregation. There is always a journey toward the self and a journey toward the neighbor in pastoral care within the context of community. The journey toward the self involves one's own questions, struggles, brokenness, sinfulness, problems, gifts, and hopes. The journey toward the other involves recognition of these same realities in our sisters and brothers. Where are you? is the personal question. Where is your brother? is the social question. In the first the genuine self is the object of discovery. In the second the genuine other is the object of discovery. God addresses both questions to us in our tendency, on the one hand to hide, and on the other to evade. The congregation as the place of pastoral care points us to the heart of the question raised in chapter one: What does it mean for persons in the fullness of their human experience to be called together in the name of Christ in such a way that the redemptive and healing power of the gospel can be present? The interrogatives of pastoral care set the perimeters for our discussion.

Where are you? raises questions about relationships. Where are you in relationship to yourself, to God, to others, to the world in which you live and work? Do you have a place to be and to become, a place to stand and from which to move? Or are you in flight and in hiding, a stranger to yourself and cut off from significant others? To borrow the title of an off-Broadway play of a few years back, are you suffering from having "no place to be somebody?"

Who are you? raises questions about identity. Do you have a coherent sense of self? What masks do you wear and what personas do you assume to hide your true self from others? Is there enough of the "you that is you" to genuinely give and receive in the ebb and flow of human relationships? Is there a sense of becoming who you want to become or do you feel "stuck" in a you that is neither liked nor accepted? Are you who you choose to be or have you acquiesced to an identity imposed on you from others?

Why are you? raises questions about *meaning* and *purpose.* Here we stand before the mystery of our existence and seek to make sense out of the journey we take from birth to death. The road for this journey is never straight. It is difficult to see around the next bend, and sometimes we struggle to see at all. There are subterranean travels. There are labyrinthine excursions. Yet this question of "why" is intimately and profoundly connected to the "where" and the "who" of our relationships and personhood. W. H. Auden's *Christmas Oratorio* is the story of such journeys we must make in and through our humanity. As the wise men set out to "follow the star" each in turn gives a verdict on the purpose of the journey.[1]

> To discover how to be truthful now
>   Is the reason I follow this star.
> To discover how to be living now
>   Is the reason I follow this star.
> To discover how to be loving now
>   Is the reason I follow this star.

Then, in a rising crescendo of their combined chorus, they acknowledge together:

> At least we know for certain
>   that we are three old sinners,
> That this journey is much too long,
>   that we want our dinners,
>   And miss our wives, our books, our dogs,
> But have only the vaguest idea why we are what we are.

---

[1]From "For the Time Being," in W. H. Auden, *The Collected Poetry* (New York: Random House, 1945) 429-31.

To discover how to be human now
Is the reason we follow this star.

Whatever else the Christian congregation may be, surely it is the place of pastoral care in which all of us together can make this journey into the fourfold quest for truthfulness, life, love, and genuine humanness. Together, in the fullness of our humanity, we seek the highest values of the human heart and search the deepest needs of the human soul. We need not hide from nor evade the most significant personal questions, for the more honest we are with ourselves the closer we will come to the essential humanity of our brothers and sisters. Pastoral care practiced as a community is characterized by mutuality. It is not a matter of the strong stooping to help the weak, the clear-headed advising the muddled, or the healthy and sound superior condescending to the groping and broken inferior; it is a journey taken together in which there is the possibility of our being pastors and priests to each other.

Such a possibility involves both a call and a promise. The call is for us to assume again as Christians the responsibility for our vocation as priests in the world. Such a vocation will involve a learning experience for all of us—a learning to be Christ to our neighbor as Luther so boldly put it. It is a vocation to be exercised both within the congregation and outside it. The promise is that we will receive the pastoral benefits and priestly blessings of our fellow travelers. The images of bridge builder (priest) and shepherd (pastor) will help us discover the nature of this work of companionship in the way.

THE PRIESTHOOD OF ALL BELIEVERS

The concept of priesthood is as old as religion, and some form of it is practiced in all religions. The priest functions as a mediator between the divine and the human. As "go-between" the priest represents God to the people (interpreting the divine oracles) and the people to God (offering sacrifices and making petitions). Pontifex, the term for the council of priests, literally means the bridge maker.

The New Testament presents Jesus Christ as the fulfillment of all the Old Testament priestly functions. He is both high priest and sacrifice (Heb. 2:17-18; 4:14-16; 10:5-25). Priesthood in the church belongs to the whole company of the faithful (1 Pet. 2:4-10). Every Christian is a priest, and life lived through Christ in worship, fellowship, and good works is seen as sacrifice offered to God (Rom. 12:1ff.; Heb. 13:15-16). In no instance does the New Testament bestow the title of priest on any individual member of the church or on a specific order of ministry. The work of priesting belongs to the community.

If Christ is our model, and the secret of Christ is incarnation, then incarnation becomes the secret of our priesthood. The Word became flesh, the divine became human, and the priestly bridge touches both worlds. Priestly work is the incarnation of God's care and the Word of that care is to be made flesh in our flesh. As bridge building priests we are called to be rooted in two worlds in order to experience and share the redemptive and healing love of God in the immediate and concrete situations of daily life. To perform religious acts that do not touch the humanity and worldliness of the world is priestly failure. The dualism that ministers to the soul a piety that is a form of escapism rather than caring for the person in the complexities of daily living is neither biblically sound nor pastorally responsible. Likewise, priestly work that conceives of itself solely in terms of human therapy has already given up its birthright to the Christian secret of priesthood—the Word of God, the love of God, and the care of God made flesh in the flesh of the Christian brother or sister. As Bonhoeffer reminded us so many years ago, "In the presence of a psychiatrist I can only be a sick man; in the presence of a Christian . . . I can dare to be a sinner. . . . It is not lack of psychological knowledge but lack of love for the crucified Jesus Christ that makes us so poor and inefficient in brotherly confession."[2]

We must reject the notion of the "priesthood of all believers" as simply a negative slogan of Protestant anticlericalism that has

---

[2]Dietrich Bonhoeffer, *Life Together*, trans. John W. Doberstein (New York: Harper and Row, 1954) 119.

no reality within the life of the church.[3] Within the life of the congregation we can consciously begin to become what we are—every person, both men and women, priests of God. It is the only adequate priesthood in our secular world. The role of the clergy within the church will be discussed in chapter six, but it is important for clergy and laity alike to recognize that an elite few within the church cannot do what the community is called to do.

To do this work of priesting demands a new awareness and a new learning for each Christian within the congregation. Christian education will not deal solely with the objective content of our faith, but with how that faith can shape and mold us into a living priesthood in the world. It will be a learning to become what we are in order that we might do the work of mediation. The goal would not be to produce a congregation of counselors, but a community of priests.

Each Christian within the community functions as a mediator. The Christian's life is the living sacrifice that enables the immediate life situation to become the altar of praise and the place of mediation. Where chasms exist bridges will be built. Where ties are broken mending will occur. Where relationships are alienated connections will be made. The Word of God and the words of men and women will have their interchange in priestly mediation. The sacramental will be present to daily life and daily life will be experienced sacramentally. When each Christian functions as a priest in the world of ordinary human life, God can be taken seriously before the world and each person can be taken seriously before God. Before we ask how this priesthood might be lived out in practical terms let us turn our attention to that other image of companionship in the way—the image of the shepherd and the sheep.

---

[3]See Hans Küng, *The Church*, trans. Ray and Rosaleen Ockenden (New York: Sheed and Ward, 1967) 363-87, for an illuminating discussion of "the priesthood of all believers" from a theological perspective by a Roman Catholic.

THE PASTORHOOD OF ALL BELIEVERS

One of the fundamental images of the relationship between God and God's people is the image of the shepherd and the sheep. A passage such as Ezekiel 34:11-16 not only reflects this image but gives as clear a description of the nature of pastoral care as can be found anywhere.

> For thus says the Lord God: Behold, I, I myself will search for my sheep, and will seek them out. As a shepherd seeks out his flock when some of his sheep have been scattered abroad, so will I seek out my sheep; and I will rescue them from all places where they have been scattered on a day of clouds and thick darkness. And I will bring them out from the peoples, and gather them from the countries, and will bring them into their own land; and I will feed them on the mountains of Israel, by the fountains, and in all the inhabited places of the country. I will feed them with good pasture, and upon the mountain heights of Israel shall be their pasture; there they shall lie down in good grazing land, and on fat pasture they shall feed on the mountains of Israel. I myself will be the shepherd of my sheep, and I will make them lie down, says the Lord God. I will seek the lost, and I will bring back the strayed, and I will bind up the crippled, and I will strengthen the weak, and the fat and the strong I will watch over; I will feed them in justice.

Ezekiel pronounces the judgment of God upon the unfaithful shepherds of Israel and depicts God as the true good shepherd whose sole concern is with the needs and health of his flock. The pastorhood of God is made flesh in the Incarnation, and Jesus lays claim to the title of good shepherd.

> I am the good shepherd. The good shepherd lays down his life for the sheep. He who is a hireling and not a shepherd, whose own the sheep are not, sees the wolf coming and leaves the sheep and flees; and the wolf snatches them and scatters them. He flees because he is a hireling and cares nothing for the sheep. I am the good shepherd; I know my own and my own know me, as the Father knows me and I know the Father; and I lay down my life for the sheep. And I have other sheep, that are not of this fold; I must bring them also, and they will heed my voice. So there shall be one flock, one shepherd (John 10:11-16).

Again, the sole concern of the shepherd is the health and safety of his sheep.

Taken together the passages from Ezekiel and John form a decisive picture of the work of shepherding. When we ask what we are to be about within the congregation as a place of pastoral care, the mandate is unmistakable: seeking the lost, finding and incorporating into the life of the community the wanderer, binding up life's wounded, strengthening the weak, pursuing justice, knowing the person, showing faithful dependability, and laying down our life for others. These concerns form the priorities for the ordering of life within the Christian congregation.

While it is true that the term pastor is ascribed to a particular function within the church, it is equally important to recognize that the community itself can function pastorally.

> The primary reference of the shepherd image is to Jesus' self-sacrificial love, which seeks a response from *every* one of his followers. Leaders and teachers of congregations have no special prerogatives in this central meaning of shepherding. We must learn to speak of the *pastorhood of all believers* and to explore the idea that *each* person has a call to lead in that special way characteristic of the Good Shepherd.[4]

We must also learn that the structuring of our life together can enable person to person pastoral care to occur both within the congregation and for those who, as Jesus put it, "are not of this fold." Our preaching and our worship, our Bible classes and our discussions, our fellowship and our service, our outreach and our missions will be designed to speak to the foundational questions of human existence rather than to the peripheral questions of religious trivia. Where are we? Who are we? Why are we? Does what we are, do, think, study, and say help heal the wound in existence and cast God's light in our present darkness? Do our structures and forms contribute to the possibility of our exploring together the

---

[4]Alistair V. Campbell, *Rediscovering Pastoral Care* (London: Darton, Longman and Todd, 1981) 31.

fundamental questions of truth, life, love, and humanity? Or do our structures and forms aid and abet our tendency toward hiding and evading?

An important paradox must, however, be recognized at the very beginning. Just as Jesus is both high priest and sacrifice, he is also both shepherd and Lamb of God. As Christians we are *both* sheep and shepherds. We *are* the lost, the wounded, and the wanderers. At the same time we are called to the pastoral responsibilities of the shepherding task. Pastoral care thus flows from the authenticity of our personhood in Christ rather than from the authority of our office in the church, from our courage based on faith in God rather than from our correctness based on our imagined righteousness, and from our vulnerability rather than from our invincibility. No less important than these three qualities are the marks of the ministry of the Lamb of God who was also the good shepherd of our souls: his authenticity, his courage, and his vulnerability.

In five areas our priestly work and pastoral care can begin to become a reality within our congregations. In these areas the fullness of our human experience can be exposed to the redemptive and healing power of God. As we priest and pastor each other within the context of our community and in light of our faith, we will be making the journey toward the discovery both of ourselves and of our sisters and brothers. In the grace that is shared along the way the revelation of God can occur. Both our personal identity and the identity of our community will be shaped and reshaped as we explore the who, where, and why of our lives and the life of the church.

Our priestly and pastoral work will involve the following ministries:

1. The ministry of story-telling—knowing ourselves and others in light of God's story.
2. The ministry of pain-sharing—bearing and being borne in light of God's suffering.
3. The ministry of confession-hearing—giving and receiving forgiveness in light of God's grace.

4. The ministry of person-freeing—bondage and freedom in light of God's acts of liberation.
5. The ministry of faith-planting—believing and doubting in light of God's call.

STORY-TELLING

Let us begin with this matter of story-telling, for it forms the basis of all other aspects of pastoral care. Why is it we so often meet as strangers? To be sure, we may know the other's name, the other's occupation, the other's interests and hobbies. We may know any number of "facts" about one another. Yet we may remain strangers. Could it be that we are strangers to *ourselves*, fearful of meeting ourselves without defense? Could it be because most others are objects of our projections, and as such, subject to our control, rather than subjects of their own lives that might require a movement of responsibility from us within any genuine meeting? Or could it be that if we really allow another *that* close to the "me that is me," we fear the prospects of rejection because we don't measure up? Could it be that we might have to stop our one-upmanship game playing, cease our pretensions, and abdicate our power? Or could it be that we fear we might not be good enough for the church, for God? We have forgotten our gospel!

If we are to answer the where, who, and why of our lives—the questions about relationships, identity, and meaning—then surely we must begin by telling stories. By story-telling we simply mean a narrative account of those events that make up our life history *and* our feelings about and interpretations of this history of who we are. Since our personal identity is formed not only by what has happened to us but also by how we perceive and understand what has happened, it is vital to look carefully at both our experience and our interpretations of that experience. Not only is it necessary for me to tell you my story if *you* are to know me, it is necessary for me to tell you my story in order for me to know *myself*. If we are to mediate grace to one another, if we are to know forgiveness and acceptance, if we are to make room for change and growth and discovery, if there is to be a possibility for genuine conversion, if we are to experience authentic relationships with

others, if we are to move beyond cursory understandings of ourselves and others, then the hearing and telling of our stories is essential to the work of pastoral care.

As we tell our stories and hear the stories of others, however,
it is not just a matter of recalling the events and happenings of our
lives. Every story is understood by means of the interpretations
we have given to the raw data of our personal histories. Our identity, the understanding of our relationships, and the meaning or
sense of significance we give to our lives depend on how we have
interpreted the material our memories have given us of the past.[5]
We tell our stories not just for the purpose of exhibitionism or
pseudo-self-disclosure but in order to clarify who we are, where
we want to go, and why. It is to give us a means of dealing with
our past and preparing us for the future.

More than likely it is the dark recesses of our lives where the
"monsters" live that most need to be exposed to the light of the
gospel if acceptance, healing, and transformation are to occur.
Ironically, it is most often "in the church" that we fear to allow
this to happen. If we cannot give serious attention to our stories
within the context of Christian community, is it any wonder that
the church and its story have little significant impact on the interpretation of our personal identity? Our identity may be far more
powerfully shaped and interpreted by the myths, values, and
symbols of business success, educational achievement, professional expertise, and the general cultural milieu than by the story
of the Christian gospel. If our personal identity is indeed to be
Christian, then our personal stories and the means by which we
interpret them must encounter the story of the God of the gospel.
This intersection of stories will be a continual process, for as the
priest in Graham Greene's Monsignor Quixote says, "I doubt if
anyone is ever fully converted."[6]

---

[5]See George W. Stroup, The Promise of Narrative Theology (Atlanta:
John Knox Press, 1981) chap. 4.

[6]Graham Greene, Monsignor Quixote (London: The Bodley Head,
1982) 29.

We have spoken of the story of the God of the gospel. The gospel is narrative. It is not a set of moralisms, ideological formulations, or philosophies. It is story. The ministry of story-telling is not, therefore, concerned only with our stories but with God's story. Not only do persons have stories, but communities have stories. When Israel spoke of her identity she told a story (see, for example, Deut. 26:5-9). It was rooted in the experience of the Exodus and interpreted as God's saving act of deliverance from bondage. Her identity was forever linked to that reality. The individual Jew's identity was interpreted in light of the communal narrative. Likewise, the church has a story that gives it its identity. It begins with Israel's story and culminates in the story of Jesus Christ, the central event being his death and resurrection. The identity of both the individual Christian and the church are linked to the narrative of Jesus Christ. Nineteen hundred years of church history is the story of the church's interpretation and appropriation of the story of Jesus Christ and the meaning of that story for different times and places.

In the ministry of story-telling—knowing ourselves and others in the light of God's story—we are involved in creating a genuine meeting point between our stories and God's story. The biblical story of God is the affirmation that at the heart of reality is love, forgiveness, meaning, and acceptance—and that all our stories are taken up in this ultimate story. My "I am" is rooted in the "I Am" of God. By seeing our stories in light of God's story we just might begin to help each other find forgiveness and wholeness. Nothing in our story is foreign to or beyond the reach of God's passionate love. When we forget our gospel we sometimes feel we must "make believe" about ourselves rather than "making faith" with the "I Am" of God. Authenticity flees the church.

Carlyle Marney did his best for years to help us see that faith is always a verb. "All 'faithing-it' is expressible in

> I am, you are, he is,
> We are, you are, they are,

with all the other forms, tenses and moods that make up the English irregular verb."[7] When Moses wants to know the name of the God who is sending him to the confrontation with Pharaoh, God answers "I am who I am" (Exod. 3:14). Salvation by grace through faith is the affirmation that the "I Am" of God meets our own "I am." Paul adds, "This is not your own doing, it is the gift of God" (Eph. 2:8). It is the total person that God loves and forgives, not just this or that part. Yet, as Marney says, we keep trying to put direct objects to our verbs of being[8]—I am a pastor, she is a doctor, you are a salesman, he is neurotic, she is immoral. Recall the story of the prostitute who anoints Jesus' feet at the house of Simon the Pharisee (Luke 7:36-50). Simon is concerned that Jesus ought to know what kind of person she is—she is a sinner. Jesus is concerned that she is. She is concerned that she is present to Jesus as she is. The story ends: "Your faith has saved you; go in peace."

Too often our use of direct objects is a means of either camouflaging who we are or seeking self-justification through what we do or have. It also means that we pigeonhole persons, place value solely on functions, relate to individuals through roles, and pass moral judgments on actions with impunity. But it is my being that God loves, and according to the Christ story, that is exactly where Christ meets me. We had it right in the old hymn: "Just as I am, without one plea"—without direct objects. What is needed, but most often lacking within the church, is a context and means for this theological affirmation to become an existential reality.

Through the ministry of story-telling and hearing we can help one another reach for that experience and come as we are to the Christ story. It is this grace that we mediate in our priesthood to each other. Eugene Peterson, in one of the best books to appear in recent years on pastoral care, warns us that the point of "making a story" together is not to twist our stories into happy endings but to hear them as true and to find a usable truth to enable us to continue the "writing" of our stories.[9]

---

[7]Carlyle Marney, Priests to Each Other (Valley Forge PA: Judson Press, 1974) 36.

[8]Ibid., 38.

[9]Eugene H. Peterson, Five Smooth Stones for Pastoral Work (Atlanta: John Knox Press, 1980) 78.

The goal of bringing our story and the Christ story together is threefold. First, there is the *recovery* of our history—the good, the bad, and the ugly—through confession. We really no longer need to pretend. Secondly, there is *reinterpretation,* which is radical conversion to the good news of the gospel. Christ really does meet us as we are and where we are and loves us still. Finally, there is *reentry* into the ambiguities of life through commitment to the ultimate story that gives our lives significance. In this process, painful though it may be, we are moving toward the discovery of who we are and who Christ is (identity), why we are and why he is (meaning), and where we are and where he is (relationships and responsibilities). Truth, life, love, and humanity really are the issues.

Perhaps much of what we are trying to say was pictured most vividly in one of the final scenes of the musical *Godspell.* During the Last Supper Jesus moves personally to each of the disciples, holding a mirror to their faces. He begins to remove the makeup, the grease paint, and the clown masks. They can now be who they are in his presence. The gift of himself to them includes the gift of their true selves to themselves. They no longer need the pretense of the games they play, for they know who they are, why they are, and where they are.

The formation of Christian identity affects very directly what we do and the use of what we have. But our doing and our having flow out of our being. For too long we have tried to validate who we are by what we do and what we have. It is no wonder we are strangers to ourselves and others.

To provide this companionship in the hearing and telling of our stories, two things will be required of us—availability and vulnerability. It would be well if in our congregational life we *did* less in order that we might *be* more. Time is the indispensable factor in story-telling if there is to be caring, catharsis, and clarifying. Antoine de Saint Exupery's *The Little Prince* beautifully illustrates the need for availability.

> The fox gazed at the little prince for a long time. "Please tame me," he said.

> "I want to, very much," the little prince replied. "But I have not much time. I have friends to discover, and a great many things to understand."
>
> "One only understands the things one tames," said the fox. "Men have no more time to understand anything. They buy things already made at the shops. But there is no shop anywhere where one can buy friendship, and so men have no friends any more. If you want a friend, tame me."
>
> "What must I do to tame you?" asked the little prince.
>
> "You must be very patient," replied the fox. "First you will sit down at a little distance from me—like that—in the grass. I shall look at you out of the corner of my eye, and you will say nothing. . . . But you will sit a little closer to me every day."[10]

To be available, patient, and a careful and concerned listener is to impart a sense of worth to your sister or brother and to help bring into focus what might otherwise be an opaque jumble of disconnected events. Our purpose as listener is not to preach, manipulate, give advice, provide solutions, or pass moral judgment. We are hearers of the word. If we cannot hear the word of a brother or sister whom we have seen it is doubtful that we can hear the word of God whom we have not seen.

We must also become vulnerable or no genuine communication or community can occur. In a sense it is illogical to speak of "becoming" vulnerable. To be alive is to be vulnerable.

> How exquisite and how perfect is the living flower which knows both birth and dying: while the plastic flower which lasts a thousand years is ever brutal in its changelessness. The softness of one and the hardness of the other. It is vulnerability that makes one open and beautiful. And surely without death there is no vulnerability.[11]

Yet we spend an immense amount of energy hiding our vulnerability. In the process of turning our gospel upside down we have

---

[10]Antoine de Saint Exupery, *The Little Prince*, trans. Katherine Woods (New York: Harcourt, Brace and World, 1943) 83-84.

[11]From the poet, Richard Shannon, quoted in Alistair V. Campbell, *Rediscovering Pastoral Care*, 40.

valued power rather than powerlessness, strength more than weakness, invincibility over vulnerability, and supremacy in place of servanthood. To tell our stories in honesty is to be vulnerable. Obviously, the congregation is not the place to tell everything to everybody, but it should provide the context for a person to tell everything to somebody. The attempt to hide our vulnerability may be why we have plastic churches rather than living churches—"the softness of one and the hardness of the other. . . . It is vulnerability that makes one open and beautiful."

In the ministry of story-telling the congregation can become the place where our stories meet, are taken up into God's story, and are given eternal significance. A gospel that does not redeem the totality of our experience is a gospel too small for our allegiance.

PAIN-SHARING

Wherever two or three are gathered in Christ's name the meeting is always in the shadow of the cross. Our ministry becomes one of pain-sharing—bearing and being borne in light of God's suffering. Yet much popular Christianity views suffering as if it should not be, promising instead a facile faith in face of brutal experience. We have been schooled in the avoidance of suffering rather than in endurance. The hawkers and hucksters of "happy talk" Christianity promise not the biblical "joy that comes in the morning," but the neon-lit artificial glare that refuses to recognize there is a night.

Pain, suffering, affliction, hurt, loss, and tragedy are universal human realities. Though universal they are experienced personally. Just as they can be found on any twenty feet of street the world over, they will be found in some form in any hundred pounds of human flesh. In that person next to you as within yourself there is suffering, has been suffering, will be suffering. We cannot avoid it. The human story and the God story cannot be told without it. Pastoral care in the Christian congregation involves engaging suffering rather than "fixing it" or trying simply to eliminate it. The redemption of suffering is at the heart of the Christian gospel, not the refusal of suffering. To ask what suffering means to us is to probe what suffering means to God. Here we are concerned with our priesthood of pain-sharing.

It is important initially to take note of various kinds of suffering. There is physical pain. It may come about through accident, injury, illness, deformity. Some forms of suffering we may bring on ourselves. Other forms of suffering bear no relationship to anything we have done. The rain falls on the just and the unjust. Nature is fundamentally indifferent to us.

Then there is the kind of suffering that seems to rise up from the very earth of our human existence. There is the anguish of the broken heart. There is the loneliness of separation through death or loss or rejection. There are the terrible emotional scars of psychic pain and mental agony. There is often the seeming triumph of evil over good. There is the horror and pain of our own guilt and sinfulness. There is the haunted suffering of anxiety and meaninglessness that leaves us empty and at the heart of darkness.

Finally, there is what Simone Weil has called affliction. Diogenes Allen points to Weil's work as "one of the most profound analyses of the nature of affliction." Affliction, according to her, involves not primarily physical suffering, but being uprooted from the fabric of social relations, no longer counting for anything, being socially degraded, and feeling inwardly the contempt and disgust that others express toward one who is socially of no account.[12]

The true priest, then, does not look for a place to hide from suffering but for a way to enter the world of the sufferer. The courage of the shepherd is here put to the test. Perhaps our most important question with regard to entering the world of the sufferer is to ask what suffering does to a person. Between what suffering does to a person and the possible responses to suffering is the bridge we are concerned with building in this priestly work of pain-sharing. We must be concerned not only with what happens *to* us but with what happens *in* us.

---

[12]Diogenes Allen, "Suffering at the Hands of Nature," *Theology Today* 37 (July 1980): 188.

The answer to the question of what suffering does *to* a person depends somewhat on the nature or the kind of suffering. But, in general, suffering or pain can create a situation in which the immediate circumstance takes precedence over normal routine, order is reduced to chaos, and altered status replaces continuity in personal story line. This can produce some or all of the following conditions within the sufferer: a sense of isolation, a feeling of entrapment, the experience of absolute powerlessness in face of threatening forces, and inescapable fear. The sufferer often feels reduced and paralyzed. The Psalmist speaks of the experience as a wasting.

> I am in distress, my eye is wasted from grief, my soul and my body also. For my life is spent with sorrow, and my years with sighing; my strength fails because of my misery, and my bones waste away. I am the scorn of all my adversaries, a horror to my neighbors, an object of dread to my acquaintances; those who see me in the street flee from me. I have passed out of mind like one who is dead; I have become a broken vessel (Ps. 31:9-12).

The sufferer is often struck dumb in the experience of suffering. The sigh, the groan, and the cry were invented for such times and are integral parts of human expression. Pious platitudes and programmatic panaceas are no cure for human anguish. To the contrary, they are means by which we try to evade, and that in itself contributes to the sense of desolation felt by the sufferer. The lament, "Is it nothing to you, all you who pass by? Look and see if there is any sorrow like my sorrow" (Lam. 1:12), is a profound plea to be given the first attention of priestly work.

So within the Christian congregation we begin making room for the sufferer by acknowledging the reality of the darker dimensions of life with the affirmation that it is especially in those dimensions that God meets us. The God of the Bible is no unmoved mover or abstract principle or universal power broker. God is a passionate God whose heart is love. God "does not stand outside the range of human suffering and sorrow. He is personally involved in, even stirred by, the conduct and fate of man."[13] We so

---

[13]Abraham Heschel, *The Prophets*, 2 vols. (New York: Harper and Row, 1962) 2:4.

quickly want to rush toward victory that we fail to see the depth
and nature of defeat. We crave healing but refuse to take time and
patience over our wounds. If we genuinely desire the healing and
redeeming power of God in the midst of our anguish then it is time
we recognize that it comes through *God's* anguish. It is not by the
power but by the wounds of God that we are healed (Isa. 53:3-5).
Person to person we say, "I do see your sorrow and it is something
to me. Let us make it a shared grief because you are important to
me. Let us take time over it. I will not abandon you; you can count
on that. Let us live through it together." Obviously this is not done
simply by making this speech. In relationship to suffering "answers" must be lived out more than spelled out. If the "why" of
suffering remains a mystery, the "who" does not. Our task in the
Christian community is to see that the "who," the sufferer, is seen
and held. By so doing we can begin to break through the isolation,
to some extent enter the prison, and at least be present to the fear.
We are saying to the sufferer, "You are not alone; you matter to
me, to us." Such a ministry humanizes suffering.

Eugene Peterson gives a profound analysis of the pastoral work
of engaging suffering.[14] Among a number of helpful insights he
gives is his insistence on the importance of anchoring suffering in
history, helping people to place a terminus on suffering, and discovering paths of deliverance in history. He points out that if suffering is severed from historical data (naming the cause of
suffering, pointing to the hour of loss, finding the "datable event"
behind suffering) it diffuses like gas filling a room. Anchoring
suffering in history binds the suffering to the particular event
rather than allowing it to diffuse, color, sour, choke, reduce, and
injure all of life. There is a tendency when we suffer to think that
since *this* painful thing has happened, *everything* is terrible. The
pastoral task is to say, "No. *This* is what has happened. Let us
spend time over *it* and suffer *it*. And let us then allow it to assume
its place among other realities."

Likewise, as we share the pain with the sufferer, Peterson
points out that we should avoid becoming "accessories to neu-

---

[14]Peterson, *Five Smooth Stones*, chap. 3.

rotic responses" by allowing evil, guilt, injury, and suffering to become an obsession.[15] We priest toward healing by taking every dimension of the suffering seriously and then by pointing to the end of something and the beginning of something else. Having "seen" the sufferer, we eventually must help the weary eyes of the sufferer to see again toward the future.

Finally, our priesting in suffering involves praying with the sufferer. It is "out of the depths" that we cry to the Lord (Ps. 130:1). As Athanasius is reported to have said, "The Psalms have a unique place in the Bible because most of scripture speaks to us, while the Psalms speak *for* us."[16] In the Christian congregation we often speak *to* each other more than *for* each other. It is crucial in bearing one another's sufferings that we speak for each other in prayer. Here we bind our hearts to the heart of God, removing our suffering from blind fate. Nature may be indifferent to us, but God is not.

> Remember my affliction and my bitterness, the wormwood and the gall. My soul continually thinks of it and is bowed down within me. But this I call to mind, and therefore I have hope: the steadfast love of the Lord never ceases, his mercies never come to an end; they are new every morning (Lam. 3:19-23).

In Christian community we do not pretend there is no night. But we do wait for the slow, sure tread of the dawn.

CONFESSION-HEARING

"Confess your sins to one another and pray for one another, that you may be healed" (James 5:16). The ministry of confession-hearing involves the Christian community in judgment and salvation. The point of this spiritual discipline is our healing and wholeness. Yet it is rarely practiced within the Protestant congregation at a person to person level in which we are priests to each other. That it should be a part of our corporate worship there is no

---

[15]Ibid., 101.

[16]Quoted by Bernard Anderson, *Out of the Depths* (Philadelphia: Westminster Press, 1970) x.

doubt. But that it might function at a more personal level is frightening to us and seldom practiced. Could it be that in walling ourselves up with our own sins we to some extent shut out grace and forgiveness and keep in distress and disease?

To make confession of sin to another—or to hear it from another—is also a ministry of pain-sharing. But it is a particular kind of pain. Here we are not dealing with pain inflicted on us, but with pain that rises within us because of our own pride, self-centeredness, weakness, and willfulness. In the confession of sin we acknowledge where we have acted against the love of God, where we have contributed to the shattering of human community, where there has been a violation or a neglect that might have affected two or more people, or where we have rebelled against God and find ourselves guilty. Sin and forgiveness are realities as are judgment and grace. Somehow in our theology we have allowed a wedge to be driven between judgment and salvation as if we needed to balance one off against the other. Or we find ourselves under the pain of constant judgment or the banality of meaningless grace. In the practice of confession they can be brought together so that "we might be healed." We are not saved so much *from* judgment as *through* judgment. Jesus did not come to make light of sin but to bear the burden of it. His cross does not mean that judgment is unnecessary but that forgiveness is possible. In the shallowness of our age we find ourselves without the depth to experience either reality with much significance.

The practice of person to person confession enables the Christian congregation to become a more truly sacramental community. A sacrament is, of course, an outward and visible sign of an inner and spiritual grace. Confession, as a sacrament, involves the incarnation of the experience of judgment and forgiveness. It is the enfleshment of God's forgiveness and delivers us from dealing with our sins merely in the realm of ideas. By objectifying the realities of sin, judgment, and forgiveness we are no longer left to the whims of our subjective feelings. Our brother/sister priest speaks to us the forgiveness of our sins in the name of Christ and incarnates the care and compassion of grace.

It is the whole church, the whole community which bears the authority to forgive sins. Matthew 18:18 itself, and the whole context of instruction to the disciples, indicates that the whole community of disciples is addressed here. . . . The whole fellowship of Jesus' disciples considers itself empowered to forgive sins, as also to administer baptism and celebrate the Lord's Supper, since the spirit has been given to it as a whole. It is in the community, as Matthew 18:20 goes on immediately afterwards to point out, that the Lord is present: 'Where two or three are gathered in my name, there am I in the midst of them!'[17]

In confession a social structure is now present. We are no longer left on our own hoping against hope for forgiveness, struggling in the loneliness of our own conscience. There before us in the flesh of our sister or brother is the concrete word of Christ—"Your sins are forgiven."

A thoughtful practice of confession can also lead to the renewal not only of the individual Christian's life, but also the life of our congregations. Renewal comes to the church not through programs, techniques, fads, pep rallies, and gimmicks, but through metanoia—repentance in response to the good news of the gospel. Bonhoeffer perceived that genuine renewal and authentic fellowship rarely occur because we have fellowship with one another only as the pious and the devout, not as the undevout, as sinners.

The pious fellowship permits no one to be a sinner. So everyone must conceal his sin from himself and from the fellowship. We dare not be sinners. Many Christians are unthinkably horrified when a real sinner is suddenly discovered among the righteous. So we remain alone with our sin, living in lies and hypocrisy. The fact is that we are sinners! But it is the grace of the gospel, which is so hard for the pious to understand, that it confronts us with the truth and says: You are a sinner, a great, desperate sinner; now come, as the sinner you are, to God who loves you. He wants you as you are; He does not want anything from you, a sacrifice, a work; He wants you alone.[18]

---

[17]Küng, The Church, 332-33.

[18]Bonhoeffer, Life Together, 111.

In confession we can begin to be personally and corporately what we already are but pretend too often we are not—namely sinners who are being redeemed. Only as such can we accept both the judgment and the grace of God and be saved from a heretical, bifurcated gospel of damnation and perpetual guilt on the one side or a self-righteous but thoughtlessly trite Christianity on the other. The confession of our sins to a brother or sister can lay an axe to the root of our pride which, in the final analysis, is the driving force behind either our self-flagellation or our self-righteousness.

Here again we argue not for a kind of indiscriminate confession of sin to everyone nor for the practice of confession as a work of righteousness. Rather, God's gift of fellowship is to grant us a brother or sister who can be our priest and to whom we can be a priest. In this way no one is forced to remain alone with their sin.

Neither is this a matter of an "inferior" seeking out a "superior." All ground is level at the foot of the cross, and it is only by standing under the cross that we can either make or hear the confession of sin. For it is under the cross that we know the cost of sin and perceive ourselves as sinners. There in that shadow (or is it light?) a word is spoken that pierces the silence of personal pain and the cacophony of social derision—"Father, forgive them." Here, in this one phrase, is the word of the cross. It is the basis of our gospel. It is the ground of our hope. It is the seed of our resurrection. It is the life force of our renewal. It is no wonder that when the disciples are told to forgive infinitely they ask not for the growth of tolerance but for the increase of faith (Matt. 18:21-22, Luke 17:3-5).

PERSON-FREEING

In however many countless hours of pastoral conversations we have had with people across the years, and in whatever we have learned from them, about ourselves as well as about them and about human experience in general, an underlying theme has constantly been a sense of bondage, entrapment, captivity, and imprisonment—in short, the lack of possibilities for life. The shackles that bind us are many and varied, strong and painful.

Bondage is a fundamental category of description about the human condition.

The biblical narrative itself is told in terms of oppression and liberation, bondage and freedom. At the heart of the biblical doctrine of redemption are the liberating acts of God. He calls men and women to freedom—from the slavery of Egypt, from the bondage of sin, from the tyranny of legalism, from the strong arms of death. The message is clear.

> Thus says the Lord, the God of Israel, 'Let my people go' (Exod. 5:1).
>
> He has sent me to proclaim release to the captives . . . to set at liberty those who are oppressed (Luke 4:18).
>
> We are not children of the slave but of the free woman. For freedom Christ has set us free. Stand fast, therefore, and do not submit to the yoke of slavery (Gal. 4:31-5:1).

However, the forces of death and bondage are not finished yet. They are set in strong array against us. We often submit to the yoke of slavery in its many forms, preferring law to gospel, the fleshpots of Egypt to the rigors of freedom, and the familiar cell to the adventurous and demanding journey. Well, we do and we don't. We are caught in a mighty contradiction.

To priest and pastor each other in companionship on the road to freedom is the task of the Christian congregation. "This is the goal of our Christian years of Christian community in Christian education: *to untie the man Christ Jesus freed,*" wrote Carlyle Marney.[19] What are our prisons? What does it mean in practical terms to be set free from the law of sin and death? Most of our prisons are constructed from the bars of the ordinary—from the circumstances of our existence in which we cannot seem to find life.

Take "time," for instance. Some of us are prisoners of our past. We have never gotten over our childhood; we are not able to utter a responsible "yes" to our adulthood. Others of us are captives of the future. Life is always out there somewhere in the future. When this or that happens, then we'll start to live. But the future has a

---

[19]Marney, *Priests to Each Other,* 80.

way of never arriving. Then again, some of us may be in bondage to the present. The servitude of the present is the experience of life as a kind of treadmill. We can just manage to get through the day, but there is no thought for the point of our frenzied activity or our drudgery filled boredom. We may well want to change our modes of behavior but cannot find the way to freedom from the bondage of time. It dominates us. Each of the modes of time, as Paul Tillich put it, has its peculiar anxiety.[20]

There is also the bondage of religion. Its forms are myriad. Much of the biblical story is written out of a liberation movement against bad religion. This bondage takes peculiar forms. We may simply be trapped by a religion that is too restrictive, that warps the truth of our humanity, that is guilt-producing without being grace-inducing, that fires all the dead wood of our hateful prejudices, or that binds us in a life-denying legalism. Or we may rebel against all the evil perpetrated in the name of religion, only to find ourselves exiled in a wasteland of no religious sensitivities whatever, unable to bear to entertain a religious question. In either case we are hardly free.

There is also a cultural bondage—those myths of our particular social order that feed our racism, our sexism, our nationalism, and our materialism. Here we are trapped in our own ideology. We are determined more by cultural expectations and values than by either our own free choice or the Christian gospel. It is our cultural bondage that often contributes to the economic, military, racial, and sexual oppression of others while at the same time insidiously blinding us to that reality. If in our pastoral care in Christian congregations we can begin to find liberation from cultural bondage and blindness, pastoral care itself may be freed from being a tool for the accommodation of people to unjust structures and may contribute instead to the broader work of liberation in society.

Of course, there is always simply the bondage to the self. Here we live with fears that traumatize us, guilts that immobilize us, greeds that trivialize us, and pride that isolates us. To be aban-

---

[20]Paul Tillich, *The Eternal Now* (London: SCM Press, 1963).

doned to the prison of the self is the loneliest, and perhaps ultimately, most terrifying bondage of all.

There are times we are aware of our bondage and long to be set free. At other times we scarcely know we are in captivity. The Christian congregation can be the place that makes it possible to speak the truth that sets us free. Unfortunately, it can also be the place where the truth is muffled. When we function in such a way that people are manipulated rather than set free, we have fallen again into the yoke of slavery. Too often this has been the case. This forms the dark side of our history. The gospel itself must at times be set free from the terrible propensity of religious authorities to bind it. To pastor each other through the priesthood of all believers toward freedom in Christ can facilitate both the freeing of persons within the congregation and freeing the liberating word of the gospel from those who would tend to domesticate it—including ourselves. But here we are concerned with the freeing of persons. How might we go about such a ministry?

If we forge our freedom on the anvil of our illusions we merely create the shape of a new and stronger bondage. Our initial quest for freedom begins with the recognition of the limits of our freedom. That is, we cannot really be free until there is a recognition and acceptance of the finitude of our humanity. False expectations, like false images of ourselves, can create a prison of unhappiness. We are partially determined by our bodily existence, by our past, by our relationships, by our future death. Freedom is to be found in and through these determining forces, not in acting as if they did not exist.

The first pastoral act toward freeing one another is the conscious and deliberate examination of the world as each of us experiences it in our personal and unique situation. If story-telling is a cathartic act that helps us discover the images that have shaped our identity, the priestly work of person-freeing clarifies our situation in life so that the liberating work of Christ may become a part of our response to our past, our present, and our future. Freedom is more an action than a possession, belonging to the verbs rather than the nouns of our existence. Metaphorically, to "visit those in prison" is to enter the stuffy, closed up rooms of a person's life in order to ask questions, probe alternatives, discover possibilities. It is to incarnate the word of possibility in the imprisoning cycle of the world of stimulus/response. It is to throw open some windows in the stifling atmosphere of the conditioned reflexes we are prone to make in our bondage.

One result of prolonged bondage is often the death of a person's imagination. The Old Testament gospel of the Exodus and the New Testament gospel of the death and resurrection of Christ form the Christian affirmation that the limits of the present do not determine the limits of the future. Expectation is the driving force of hope. To enter into a pastoral relationship with creative imagination where imagination has died is to give sight to the blind. Without hope we are in fact hopeless. The priestly work of person-freeing is to enter into relationships in which the future appears to be closed, to speak and act in hope, and to work with patience to help people actualize the possibilities of freedom.

From the Christian perspective the ultimate act of freedom is the act of faith. In faith a person makes a fundamental commitment in the midst of the necessities of life and death. It was the faith of Jesus that gave him the freedom to live and die. And our freedom is a freedom in and through Christ. "For the law of the spirit of life in Christ has set me free from the law of sin and death" (Rom. 8:2). The prison doors have been opened. Through the nurturing of faith in pastoral care we seek the courage to participate in the freedom already won, actualizing it in the ordinary affairs of daily living. In the grammar of faith we are given the syntax of freedom—to be the subjects rather than the objects of the verbs of life.

FAITH-PLANTING

The goal of our common priesthood is our growth toward the wholeness and authenticity of our personhood in Christian maturity. In our mutual pastoral care we seek the answer of faith to the who, where, and why questions of our existence. Our work is never directed solely inwardly for two reasons. The first is that we seek our life in God, who has taken on our humanity in Jesus, yet remains wholly other. The second is that we seek not only our own felicity, but that of our neighbor also.

The very source of our Christian existence is faith. "For I am not ashamed of the gospel: it is the power of God for salvation to every one who has faith, to the Jew first and also to the Greek. For in it the righteousness of God is revealed through faith for faith; as it is written, 'He who through faith is righteous shall live'" (Rom. 1:16-17). Faith and life are the content and context of our priesthood. The only reason for the existence of the Christian congregation is that it has heard the story of Jesus Christ and has been called into being by his word. God's word spoken in Jesus Christ is the call to life. Now as in the days of the Galilean ministry that call is heard, if it is heard at all, in the midst of the ordinary and daily routine of living. For this reason pastoral care is the ministry of faith-nurturing in light of God's call.

But the concept of faith is not easy for us to understand. It is not just an intellectual formula or a body of knowledge. It is not just a subjective feeling, a kind of inner glow. It is not just a blind act of the will in which we make a leap in the dark. We do not possess it like an object nor experience it as if it were like piped-in "muzak." It is not surprising that most of us find ourselves in the position of the man in the gospel who cried out, "I believe; help my unbelief" (Mark 9:24).

Fundamentally, faith is a relationship of trust between a person (or community) and God based on the person and work of Jesus Christ. To believe in God who is made known in Jesus affects the way one sees, experiences, understands, and lives life. To believe in God is not to have all the answers nor is it to be removed from doubt, sin, or affliction. It is not to be removed from the world but to be thrust into it. It is not to be made more than human or other than human but fully human. It is to be involved in a vision of life that is large enough for life in all its dimensions and ambiguities—the dark as well as the bright, the suffering as well as the celebration, the evil as well as the good. In the end, it is a commitment, a faith/obedience that sees in Jesus Christ the truth about humanity and the values of the kingdom of God, and is willing to live, however feebly or strongly, toward their manifestation in one's life and in society. In the paradoxical way of the gospel, faith is both a gift of God and a human commitment, something one receives as well as comes to, something one is held by as well as takes hold of.

In the priestly work of nurturing faith we are taken to the heart of the truth of the Christian gospel: it is about relationships—

> broken relationships that need to be healed,
> unjust relationships that need to be corrected,
> unholy relationships that need to be forgiven,
> unloving relationships that need to be transformed,
> alienated relationships that need to be restored,
> and bound relationships that need to be freed.

The gospel is the story of the God who enters into a covenant relationship with a people, reconciling them in Christ and giving them the ministry of reconciliation (2 Cor. 5:18).

The nurturing of this faith, the heart of which is concerned with relationships (loving God and loving the neighbor), surely begins in relationships. Though he was concerned with the prospects of change through a therapeutic relationship, Carl Rogers recognized that change comes through experience in a relationship rather than through the intellect by the imparting of knowledge or the use of technique.[21] We see this principle at work in the Gospels in Jesus' call to the disciples to be "with him." Being present to the particulars of another life in his or her heart, history, and hope is the first and essential step toward the nurturing of faith and the possibility of conversion.

The nature of the relationships we have in the covenant community is defined by and connected through the living spirit of Christ. "The Holy Spirit is given to enable the 'two or three gathered together' to embody Jesus Christ in the world."[22] Our friendship in Jesus Christ is not just with one another in the fellowship of the church, but through the church with the world. The priestly

---

[21]Carl Rogers, *On Becoming a Person* (Boston: Houghton Mifflin, 1961) 33.

[22]John V. Taylor, *The Go-Between God* (London: SCM Press, 1972) 134.

work of nurturing faith takes place both within the church and outside it. In either case "being present to another" allows the presence of Jesus to be made manifest in such a way as to articulate his call to life.

For most of us our faith began by believing in the God of someone else. We do not simply arrive at faith in an isolated and objective search. Faith grows in the context of life and relationships in which the story of Jesus is a lived reality.

> The living truth is what I long to see;
> I cannot lean upon what used to be.
> So shut the Bible up and show me how
> The Christ you talk about is living now.[23]

The Bible is of course always to be open in the church, but it is not there simply as a relic for veneration or a proof-text manual for the manipulation of others. It is a living word to be taken up by the church in order that the story of Jesus might shape the story of our lives. Or, as Paul put it to the Corinthian church, "You are a letter from Christ delivered by us, written not with ink but with the spirit of the living God, not on tablets of stone but on tablets of human hearts" (2 Cor. 3:3). But often the "letters of our lives" and our life together reflect anything and everything other than the centrality of Jesus Christ in our faith.

This is why in the work of pastoral care, as well as in the church's preaching and teaching ministry, the figure of Jesus must be sought again and again along with the meaning he has for our different contexts and life situations. Nurturing faith is not simply accomplished by producing biblical snapshots of a first-century Jesus. He is the risen Lord of life and is to be sought in the living of life. The Gospels, the creeds, and the history of tradition are all important to our understanding of Jesus. But they are not substitutes for our own "I believe." Brainwashing, browbeating, indoctrination, and manipulation have no place in the priestly

---

[23]Sidney Carter, *Songs of Sidney Carter: In the Present Tense* (Norfolk, England: Galliard, 1969) 2.

work of nurturing faith. They may all lead to the acceptance of a certain set of ideas, but they do not lead to genuine faith or to the growth and development of the person in Christian maturity.

Faith is a way, a road, in which we walk. We can offer each other no more than companionship on the journey as we keep pointing to the One who has made the journey before us. It is he that is the perfecter of our faith, not ourselves (Heb. 12:2). This obviously means faith does not fall full blown from heaven so that all of the points of Christian doctrine are assimilated, accepted, and understood. Our priesthood consists of living with the ambiguities of understandings and misunderstandings of Jesus, just as was the case with the earliest disciples. Difficulties, doubts, sins, unanswered questions, and struggles with points of Christian doctrine are not unbelief. As Luther said, "Every doctrine has its age, its time, its hour." They do not all come into focus with the same power or effect or meaning at every point of our journey. But to keep walking, to recognize that the school of faith is a lifelong learning-to-be, and to nurture trust in him who calls us in the way, these are the encouragements we offer each other in our priesthood. To live our lives in such a way as to become "reasons to believe" does not call us beyond tragedy and grief any more than it did the Lord of our faith. To attempt to reflect the love of God is not to be almighty ourselves. It is in the profound humility of our call, not in the pride of our perfection, that we make the journey of faith together.

What we have tried to picture here is a community of pastoral care where the full experience of our humanity can be suffered, interpreted, and celebrated in Jesus Christ who is present to us in our sisters and brothers. The questions of relationships, identity, and meaning must be explored and answered together. These questions never belong simply to the single individual, nor are they to be relegated to the concern of the religious professional. In this community we are not passive observers but active participants. At the same time we need only give what we have to give and be prepared to be open to receiving what we need to receive. We are priests who are priested. We are pastors who are pastored.

And all of this priesting and pastoring, like our life itself, is taken up and redeemed by the high priesthood of Christ who is the shepherd of our souls.

5

A SCHOOL
OF DISCIPLESHIP

By these deeds we confess him. . . .

Second Clement

*T*he Christian congregation lives a life called *koinonia*—
a communion in forgiveness, in suffering, in possessions, and in
the joy of loved life. This *koinonia* is the work of Christ as he
abides in even the smallest company gathered in his name. But
the congregation exists also to hand back to Christ the life it has
received. It lives to serve him, to represent him, to conform to him,
to walk and speak as his body in the world. The congregation is
also a *koinonia* in obedience. It is the place where the standard
and discipline and the imperative of Christ are maintained in the
world.

The very name congregation means a gathering, a coming together. We have been speaking of the church in its gathered form—
not simply in its formal "meetings" but in the daily meeting and
gathering of a shared life. In this sense, the church is always gathering and meeting. But gathering also presupposes dispersion,
scattering. In the lives of its members the congregation is day by
day scattered in the world. They move like leaven into the lump

of the world. They are sent out like letters from Christ to the world. Even in its most intimate meeting and planning, the congregation sees itself as scattered in the world, as a part of that *diaspora* of God that is scattered for a purpose.

The task of this dispersed people is not to fit and blend like a chameleon in the world, but to be transformed and renewed by another way and another "world." Each congregation has been sent into the world by Christ. Its piece of the world is its land of pilgrimage. In its gathering its task is to discern the voice of Christ and to obey, to see the direction Christ is traveling in this world and to follow.

But the congregations of which we are a part are not made up of heroes and heroines who relish struggle and conflict. "Obedience" and "discipleship" bring to mind unswerving loyalty and sacrifice. Can we really speak in such terms in today's churches? Are we not men and women who struggle even to believe and to love our families and closest friends? Perhaps honesty would compel us simply to be content with the term "Christian," or even "church member," denoting only the most general allegiance to Christian values.

In the four Gospels there are in fact *two* groups of people who follow Jesus: the disciples and the crowd. The disciples follow Jesus because they have recognized in him one to whom they owe allegiance; he has called them by name and they mean for their lives to be lived in his service. Those in the crowd follow for all sorts of reasons—they come for healings, for feeding, for comforting, or because he voices their own deep longings, or because here is one who speaks as if he is certain about the God in whom they only vaguely believe. In their need they follow Jesus.

Although Jesus sometimes flees the crowd, though he is burdened by its mediocrity, fickleness, and slowness to learn, he never rejects the crowd and its claims upon him. In fact, the one miracle that all four Gospels record is an action that typifies the attitude of Jesus toward the crowd.

> He saw a great throng, and he had compassion on them, because they were like sheep without a shepherd; and he began to teach them many things. And when it grew late, his disciples came to

him and said, ". . . send them away to go into the country and vil-
lages round about and buy themselves something to eat." But he
answered them, "You give them something to eat." . . . And he
commanded them all to sit down . . . and taking the five loaves
and the two fish he looked up to heaven, and blessed, and broke
the loaves, and gave them to the disciples to set before the people;
and he divided the two fish among them all (Mark 6:34-41).

The words of Christ over the bread and fish send the Christian
reader's imagination forward to the Last Supper, where Christ
himself is the food for the people (John 6 makes the connection
clear). This multitude that needs feeding foreshadows the church.
In the church there are disciples, but there is also the crowd that
Jesus will not send away and that the disciples are commanded to
serve.

The church has always been made up of these two sorts of people, the disciples and the crowd. There is no reason to assume that
this strange mixture of "strange saints" will ever be less mixed.
For the church is a home for sinners, who come to Christ not in
heroic courage and high idealism, but in various kinds of hunger,
poverty, and fear—in search of a yoke that is easy. Even as we write
about discipleship we are deeply suspicious of any conception of
the church that attempts to shut out the crowd by construing some
visible holiness, purity, or "radical" obedience as the criterion for
belonging. The Christian community does not exist by virtue of
its discipleship.

In fact, the line between the disciples and the crowd is not always easy to draw. It often cuts right across even the most dedi-
cated Christian life. It has always been so. As the Gospels tell their
story, the cross literally disintegrates the distinction between the
disciples and the crowd. In the Passion of Jesus, the disciples are
lost from view; they have faltered and run away; they have sunk
into the crowd. On the other hand, Mary Magdalene and a few
other women emerge from the crowd to serve the crucified body
of Christ, and they are the first to hear the gospel of the resurrection (Mark 15:40ff., 16:1ff.).

Yet if the stark call to obedient discipleship is not heard, if the
men and women in the crowd cannot hear the voice of Jesus calling their name, then indeed the church has become no more than

"the crowd," held together by mere dogma or a spiritless social habit. A large part of the marvel of Jesus of Nazareth—part of the mystery of his authority over lives—was his deep and vivid insight into the hurts and weaknesses of men and women, bound up with an unabashed and tireless confidence in their capacity to act like the sons and daughters of God. It was, after all, to the prostitute that Jesus said, "go and sin no more;" it was to men of no great spiritual distinction that he said, "follow me;" it was to the crowds that he preached the radical faith and costly love of the Sermon on the Mount. Under his call and in his fellowship a number of these ordinary women and men came to be the fellow-workers and the fellow-sufferers of God.

The Christian congregation does not call itself "Christian" by virtue of the obedience of its members. It lives out of the forgiving presence of Christ. But that presence is also an impelling presence, making present the word of command, a word to discomfort the complacent and transform ordinary lives with the action of a new humanity. The Christian congregation is not a holiness society, but a community called by the holy Christ. It is a school of discipleship where life is learned and relearned in the discipline of Jesus Christ.

GRACE IN OBEDIENCE

Writing to the enlightened "despisers of religion" in the seventeenth century, Pascal insisted that for many the only way to really learn to believe is first to act as if you believed. Attempt to control your passions, to care for others, to pray; even go to church! Of course, Pascal knew that reason has its say in faith, and he wrote with all his wit to convince the unbeliever. He knew as well that it is ultimately by the inspiration of God that faith comes and by nothing less. But he insisted that in the "grammar" of belief, action often leads the mind and the heart, that the doing and the willing lead the heart to truth.[1] The ultimate goal is genuine, heartfelt trust in God. But some people (and perhaps all people

---

[1]Blaise Pascal, *Pensées*, trans. A. J. Krailsheimer, Penguin Classics (Baltimore: Penguin Books, 1966) 152.

sometimes) must do faith before they think and feel it. This same relation exists between grace and obedience in Christian experience.

The very word "obedience" has come upon hard times in many (especially Protestant) Christian circles. It still carries the weight of an old Protestant/Catholic polemic. For many "obedience" calls to mind a chasing after God's favor, or thoughtless servility, or (that greatest of fears in Protestant spirituality) "works-righteousness." Obedience, it is said, is simply the by-product of faith. We must communicate the love of God in the unsolicited gift of Christ; then men and women will naturally desire to do the will of God. The Christian message is, in its simplest form, "you are accepted." And Christian faith is, in its simplest form, the acceptance of God's acceptance.

This is all true in the most profound sense; and the proclamation, "you are accepted," shatters all human pretense and pride. Further, it is certainly true that among many sectarian, Catholic, and Protestant Christians all sorts of self-justification and pride are still at work. But at the same time, and in exactly the same quarters, it is also true that the very word "grace" has been so formalized and divorced from experience that it has come to mean really no more than indulgence.

We do not always learn what is first at the beginning. We do not grasp the first truth first. The fact is that Christian truth is not readily reduced to any word, even so grand and biblical a word as "grace." In the chronology of Christian experience, the call to obedience may need to be heard before the word of grace can meaningfully be sounded. John Vincent was sensitive to the chronology of experience when he wrote, "Christ as merciful savior is a mystery and an experience belonging to the maturity of the Christian life, rather than to its initiation."[2] Is it not true that Peter and James and John called Jesus teacher and master long before they called him savior? One learns to speak before one knows the rules of grammar; one learns to walk and run before one learns

---

[2]John Vincent, *Christ and Methodism* (London: Epworth Press, 1965) 66.

anatomy. Just so, a man or woman may have to venture out on the waters with Jesus before the depth of his identity is known. Perhaps this is why Jesus consistently silenced the demons who "knew" his identity; since they could not know him in the fellowship of obedience, they could not really know him at all.

Faith, hope, and love are our life-connections to our God. But faith needs a life to rule before it needs a mind to inform. Obedience is the education of life to grace. It is grace that such obedience is demanded, and it is grace that enables us to obey.

PASSION IN POWERLESSNESS

If we look into our lives and ask about the hostility we find there to the call of Christ, we must look deeper than any formalized question of "faith versus works." There we come up against the most insidious form of hostility, the hostility of apathy. This is the great opposite of all that has to do with Jesus Christ; this is the great but subtle antagonist. Faith's true opposite is not doubt, but apathy. Hope's deadly foe is not tribulation, but apathy. Love's great enemy is not really hatred, but apathy. Joy's antithesis is not suffering, but apathy.

It is striking to recall in our present way of life the old sin *accedie*, counted by the old theologians among the seven deadly sins—alongside greed, anger (violence and aggression), lying, lust, and pride. There is no good English translation for *accedie*. It is often rendered "sloth," and sometimes "indifference" or "apathy." Originally it described the "spiritual sadness" of the monk who could neither pray nor work. Today, in the age of depth-psychology, we are eager to discern the sources of such "depressions," and we are not quick to call such conditions sinful, especially where they are judged to be "clinical." But on a wider scale, the old sin of indifference, zestlessness, the failure to act, seems to have taken on frightful proportions. The psychiatrist Karl Menninger has resurrected this old sin in his analysis of our society.

> Let it stand that there is a sin of not doing, of not knowing, of not finding out what one must do—in short of not caring. This is the

literal meaning of acedia, recognized as a sin for so many centuries, and plaguing us still.[3]

It is not difficult to understand the logic of this contemporary
version of an old sin. The growing *complexity* of our world throws
our minds and our wills into a profound ambiguity about what
"ought to be done." How often have we listened to agonized discussions among caring people about *how* one actually goes about
feeding the hungry in our society, since charity, it is said, only in-
creases dependence and fosters patronizing attitudes? The very
pace of our lives leaves many people exhausted and fraught without time or energy to be concerned about anything beyond the immediate sphere of "me and mine." And the very *scale* of the needs
around us leaves us feeling impotent and frustrated. Our knowledge far outstrips our capacity to make any difference. How can
my life, or the life of my small Christian congregation, be taken
seriously in such a world? So we lie down at night and close our
eyes, like that weary soul in Graham Greene's *The Human Factor*,
seeking not the kingdom of God, nor the kingdom of Marx, but the
kingdom of peace of mind.

No analysis, no appreciation of the odds against meaningful
action, can soften the judgment of the cross on the passionless existence of not caring and not doing. Apathy marks the stark polar
opposite to the life of Jesus Christ. The very name we give to his
sufferings—the *Passion*—means fundamentally *able to be moved.*
His life was movable, vulnerable, impressionable, in the most
profound sense. He was able to be moved by the will of God and
by the sound and sights of women and men around him.

The Christian *koinonia* has little meaning if it cannot drink and
communicate a passion for life, if it cannot serve to soften and
make life impressionable again with the passion of Christ. The
prayer we must make to Christ in our midst is an invocation of his
passion. Where Christ is, there is spoken the passionate "yes" to
life with all the duties and sacrifices such a "yes" entails. Our

---

[3]Karl Menninger, *Whatever Became of Sin?* (New York: Hawthorn
Books, 1973) 148.

obedience to Christ is our prayer for such passion. It is the most eloquent prayer we can offer. Without this prayer of our doing, the words of our prayers can hardly be uttered in good faith.

Such obedience in search of Christ's passion, born of Christ's passion, is the Christian's way through the complexities, the exhaustion, and the powerlessness that paralyze us. The small Christian community gathered in the midst of a vast urban society is the very picture of powerlessness. It is a paradox we desperately need to discern—that such powerlessness is our only real asset, which is the same as saying our only real asset is the cross of Jesus Christ.

THE DIGNITY OF THE GOOD WORK

"Today, when you hear his voice, do not harden your hearts" (Heb. 3:7). This urgent "today" is the starting place for Christian obedience; it offers to us the freedom and courage to act in the face of ambiguity and uncertainty. You cannot discern the truth and the vital need of any situation from afar; you cannot know the whole will of God at once. But, as the poet Jesus son of Sirach wrote, "Birds flock with their kind; so truth returns to those who practice it" (27:9). Every act ventured in obedience to God brings new light from God. "He who does what is true comes to the light, that it may be clearly seen that his deeds have been wrought in God" (John 3:21).

The deeds done in the light of God do not falter at their own smallness, their powerlessness, their failure to "accomplish" in the world. It is true, much that we do in the name of Jesus Christ carries little statistical weight. Christians will not eradicate hunger and suffering. They will not defeat war or quell oppression. They will not convert the world to Christ, or even prove to many the truth of their faith. Still, in all these tasks they are called to give their minds and energy and their very lives. But this giving will go on in thousands of small places. The left hand will not know what the right hand is doing, and each deed will appear to fall to the earth as some forgotten fragment. But this smallness is full of anticipation, and these fragments lie, like seeds, awaiting resurrection. None are lost, because they are kept safe by the promise of God.

Jesus had an eye for the small work and the hidden deed. When he named those actions that best represent the Son of man in the world, he spoke of giving food to the hungry, sharing a drink of water, welcoming the stranger, visiting the sick and imprisoned. In such deeds he saw signs and preparations of a new kingdom. When a woman came to do the simple honor of anointing his feet with oil, he saw the action as an anticipation of his death. When another drew him water from the well, his eyes were filled with the vision of the eternal life-giving waters of God. In their obscurity such small deeds partake of the hiddenness of Christ's own messiahship; they share in the obscurity of his sacrifice at remote Golgotha. This is their meaning, and they need no other.

The dignity of the work done in the name of Christ is that it is joined to Christ's offering to God on behalf of the world. It is a prayer offered in his name, an invocation: "Thy kingdom come, Thy will be done on earth. . . ." This coming kingdom is better prayed about than talked about. Only a fool can speak with ease about a new world. There is much darkness and suffering and much that is inexplicable. But when the believer does the truth in love, even in the face of the dark and the inexplicable, he or she learns the meaning of Peter's words about being "born again to a living hope" (1 Pet. 1:3).

The Christian hopes for the coming of the kingdom, in God's ultimate *renovatio*, in a new heaven and new earth. But the Christian nonetheless suffers ("groans," says Paul) under the contradictions and the seeming defeats. The Christian disciple groans as well when looking at the broken fragments of obedience. What we offer is far too little for the remaking of any world. We await Christ's new miracle of multiplication, writ large across all existence, when the silent offerings of his people are gathered and made whole.

THE "ENGENDERING DEED"

What does it mean to obey Jesus Christ, to follow him, to do his deeds in the world? As soon as one turns to the New Testament, it becomes clear that there is no simple, prescriptive program that every Christian community should enact. Yet we are confronted by the words and deeds of Jesus which, in the most concrete sense, define a disciple's posture in the world and provide the norm and the authority for action in the name of Jesus.

Theologians have filled volumes discussing the question of whether or not the commands of Jesus in the Gospels constitute a new Christian "law," a loosely defined ideal, or a "model." For those concerned with the reformers' doctrine of sola fide, the question was pursued with special intensity. We do not want to say that the questions of method and the nature of authority in Christian ethics are not important ones. But these theoretical questions pale before the more immediate question of how it is that we have come to a place where the words of Jesus exercise almost no concrete authority in the lives of many Christians. Surely there is a place for what one might call a "post-Reformation naivete" that asks simply, "What does Jesus demand of us; are we doing his deeds in the world?"

Of course to listen to the words of Jesus in the Christian congregation is to hear them in living connection to the sanctifying presence of the Holy Spirit and in the simply given love of the cross. In that circular language with which Karl Barth was so fond of defending the sovereign initiative of God, "Every 'Thou shalt!' and 'Thou shalt Not!' is seriously meant as an intensified indicative which has the force of an intensified imperative."[4] Or, in the simpler language of Augustine, God gives what God demands.

It is clear that the earliest known Christian ethical writing outside the New Testament, the Didache, invokes the words and commands of Jesus in defining clearly the two Ways, the Way of Life and the Way of Death. For our part, we are deeply grateful for those in the Christian tradition who have taken the words of Jesus with a life or death seriousness—for the long monastic tradition on one side and, on the other, the radical Protestant tradition that

---

[4]Karl Barth, Church Dogmatics, 4 vols. (Edinburgh: T. & T. Clark, 1957) 2, 2: 694.

bears such fruit in the work of the Mennonite Church and in many small intentional communities.

If there is no ultimate scheme or system one can build from the commands of Jesus, it is nonetheless clear that the Christian community can still discern the Way of Life and the Way of Death in the words of Jesus. In the struggles that make up our lives, it is still evident where Jesus stands and what he stands against. Each word of Jesus was spoken to particular persons in concrete situations. There is no substitute for the ongoing encounter in which the particular words of Jesus meet the particular tasks of our congregations. But we may also see in a more general way the shape of the life of discipleship. We can point to prominent spheres of concern, to definite directions, to distinct lines of action in the commands of Jesus.

Again and again Jesus speaks about our *possessions*, about *wealth* and *poverty*. Against accumulation, preoccupation, and attachment, Jesus demands from his disciples an out-flowing generosity, an almost reckless readiness to turn loose what one regards as his or her own, a sacrificial sharing, and a literal detachment. "Do not lay up for yourselves treasures on earth" (Matt. 6:19). "Give to him who begs" (Matt. 5:42). In these unambiguous words of Jesus, there is a deep suspicion and hostility toward wealth and all the anxieties such wealth produces (Mark 10:17ff.; Matt. 6:25; 19:23). Can we be genuinely together in the discipline of Jesus if our togetherness does not lead and enable us in new experiments in simplicity of life, in a more literal sharing of our possessions, in quite simply and quantitatively giving more away and keeping less for ourselves?

Again and again Jesus speaks about *power, influence, prestige*. Against all forms of power-wielding, self-exaltation, and cultivated influence, Jesus demands a "coming down," a vocation of humility in the service of others. "He who is greatest among you shall be your servant; whoever exalts himself will be humbled and whoever humbles himself shall be exalted" (Matt. 13:8-12; see also Matt. 20:26; Mark 9:35; 10:43; Luke 9:48; 22:26; 23:12). The words of Jesus cast the gravest doubts on any attempt to control or manipulate others. His own messiahship was a rejection of power in preference to love and "the form of a servant."

It is not clearly enough understood that power, influence, and prestige do not become less suspicious by being brought under the service of religious ends. Is our common life really in the way of Jesus if our congregation attempts to promote its life by way of influence and advertising and by trying to make Christianity attractive to others, like some club seeking longer registry rolls? Is there any legitimate "self-promotion" in the discipline of Jesus other than the simple act of love and straightforward truthful speech?

Again and again Jesus speaks about the apparently determinative and inalienable *human attachments*. Against a life founded on loyalty to family, nation, cause, or any self-evident grouping principle, against the philosophy of "me and mine," Jesus calls his disciples to a transcending loyalty to him and to his cause. "If anyone comes after me and does not hate his own father and mother, and wife and children, and brothers and sisters, yes, and even his own life, he cannot be my disciple" (Luke 14:26). "If your hand or your foot cause you to sin, cut it off and throw it away; it is better to enter life maimed or lame than with two hands or two feet to be thrown into eternal fire" (Matt. 18:8). Such words confirm the deep suspicion of Jesus toward any "natural" good that is cut off from the one who alone is good. Against all natural (and, therefore, naturally exclusive) human connections, Jesus preaches a new family constituted by a new transcending love and loyalty: "Whoever does the will of God is my brother, and sister, and mother" (Mark 3:35). Is our togetherness really a togetherness in Jesus if our common life does not foster lifelong relationships across unexpected lines; if such relationships do not have the force of family; and if this family loyalty does not radically qualify all other loyalties?

Again and again the words of Jesus call to mind *those who are poor* in wealth, dignity, religion, or spirit. Against a life of "upward mobility" and separation of class or religion, Jesus preaches a preferment towards the poor, calls them his brothers and sisters, and commands his followers to move among them and stand with them. "Blessed are the poor" (Luke 4:20). "As you did it to the least of these my brethren, you did it to me" (Matt. 25:40; see also Luke 16:20-25). In this partisan preference for the poor, Jesus paradoxically preaches the universal love of God. For if God's love comes first to the "undeserving" and the forgotten, all may be brought to their unworthiness before God, and so be lifted up by God. Is our togetherness really a togetherness in the name of Jesus if we cannot actively make room in our fellowship for the "outsider," if the poor, the ill, and the broken are not a visible part of our life? Can we be going the way of Jesus together if our outreach does not lead us into a new fellowship with the "least of these" brothers and sisters of Jesus?

Again and again Jesus commands his disciples to continue in prayer. Against a life of anxious scheming and planning and self-willed strategy, Jesus commands a life that flows daily from the life of God in prayer. "Ask and it will be given to you. . . . How much more will the heavenly father give the Holy Spirit to those who ask him" (Luke 11:9-13). "And he told them a parable, to the effect that they ought always to pray and not lose heart" (Luke 18:1). If we were more honest about the prayerlessness of our lives, we would more readily see that Jesus' words about prayer have the tone, not of brotherly suggestion, but of the lordly command. And if we would attend to the inherent self-centeredness in much Christian prayer, we could more readily see the urgency of maintaining the link (evident in the words of Jesus) between prayer and discipleship. Jesus commands his disciples to pray for whatever is needed, while he teaches them always "only one thing is needful." Both the assurance and the discipline are at work in the "disciples' prayer" he taught his followers to pray. The disciples are free to pray "give us," while they are taught the simplicity of "this day." And this "give us" is hedged on one side by "Thy will be done" and on the other by "deliver us from evil."

Many sorts of people pray: children pray, the seeker prays, even atheists, we believe, pray. All of these are heard in the Infinite Love about which they may know little or nothing. The tenor and structure of the disciples' prayer teaches us that for the one who prays with Jesus and in his discipline, prayer is a longing and listening for the will of God. This prayer God answers by the Holy Spirit.

The demands of Jesus seem harsh. But there ought to be no blunting of the surgical sharpness with which these words penetrate our lives. It is agonizingly difficult to know always how to hear and do them ("Lord, who then can be saved?"). But no doctrinaire appeal to grace or flight to the "inner person" can really escape the questions they ask of us. And if we wrestle with this demanding grace, which comes to us in the specific demands of Jesus, we will discover with our lives the meaning of the deed of Christ to which these demands point. For the phrase from the lips of Jesus that penetrates to the spirit of each of these demands and discloses their unity is his oft repeated "take up your cross" (Mark 8:34; Matt. 16:24ff.; Luke 9:2ff.). With his commands he shapes the lives of his disciples to conform to his cross. His cross is the "engendering deed" from which all the deeds of discipleship flow.[5]

When we locate in the cross the direction of discipleship, the meaning of Christian discipleship takes on its true proportions. For the cross is not simply the deed of Jesus. It is the very act of God who is "in Christ reconciling the world to himself" (2 Cor. 5:19). In the cross of Christ God has made the long pilgrimage of love toward his creation. Christian discipleship is not simply the imitation of a holy man, the holiest of holy men. It is an imitation of the cross-bearing God. To obey Jesus, to go the way of cross-bearing, is to recapitulate this long pilgrimage of God. It is to be conformed to the engendering deed of God in Christ.

This was for Paul the meaning of Christian baptism—a meaning that has been largely lost in the churches. Baptism is Christ's gift to his community, again, the gift that is the demand. In this concrete, bodily, visible act, the disciple's life is stamped for concrete, bodily, and visible action in the world. "All of us who have been baptized into Christ were baptized into his death . . . so that as Christ was raised by the glory of God we too might walk in newness of life" (Rom. 6:3, 4). Baptism is the community's sacrament of obedient discipleship. And the life of discipleship is a baptismal pilgrimage in the death and resurrection of Jesus Christ.

---

[5]The phrase "engendering deed" is used in this way by James M. Gustafson in *Christ and the Moral Life* (Chicago: University of Chicago Press, 1968) 174. Gustafson is discussing Joseph Sittler's *The Structure of Christian Ethics*.

DISCIPLESHIP IN COMMUNITY

We have urged that the Christian congregation is to be a school of discipleship, a *koinonia* in the words and demands of Jesus, a way of being together in which the believer is formed by the cross of Jesus for obedience in the world. But we fear this image may not yet communicate how intimately bound up is the work of discipleship with the work of Christian community. It is not as if discipleship is one work and community another. Christian discipleship creates Christian community, and such a community makes discipleship an actual possibility.

At one time in our own experience we heard the demands of Jesus with dread. They seemed to us to call for a heroic renunciation we could not achieve. His words bore down relentlessly against ambition, possessions, the privacy of family, and the cultivation of the "happy life" as we perceived it. As Christian ministers, we felt ourselves unable to echo in any sense the intensity of the gospel imperatives without great unease. When our work brought us and our families into a more intentionally shared life with other Christians at Disciples House in London (it was partly this unease about discipleship that created this shared life), certain simple concrete responses to the demands of Jesus began to come within reach. This was very unsettling as well as strangely comforting. We now found the motive to open the doors of our homes to the "skippers" on the street, since now there were others with us who shared the risk, the work, the inconvenience, and the entanglements. Now we found the incentive to move toward the simpler existence we had so often talked about, toward less ambition, toward less anxiety about the future, toward a more spontaneous and joyful response to the needs around us, because now our lives, the lives of our families, our money, our plans, were bound up with others who had covenanted with us in these matters. There came a new accountability in our lives as we were challenged by the struggles and sacrifices of our new extended family of faith. The nearness of others imposed a greater discipline in our worship, our prayers, our claims and demands. Also there came a more solid joy and a new freedom in wrestling with the imperatives of Jesus Christ.

This sketch is, no doubt, too ideal. We do not for a moment wish to make our own experience or the experience of the small community at Disciples House prescriptive for anyone else. Many Christians have less choice about their "style of life" than we have had (but more choice than they think they have). Others will simply choose another way.

But our experience together has taught us to see new possibilities for ourselves and for others. It has taught us also to recognize the inherent drive toward community in the ethic of Jesus. The demands of Jesus are meant for the community of Jesus. Their weight is meant to be borne together. The joy and freedom of their discipline is to be found together. Perhaps this is the meaning of Jesus' words to Peter:

> There is no one who has left house or brothers or sisters or mother or father or children or lands, for my sake and for the gospel, who will not receive a hundredfold now in this time, houses and brothers and sisters and mothers and children and lands, with persecutions, and in the age to come eternal life" (Mark 10:29-30).

The Christian community is the new house and new family that make Christian discipleship a possibility.

What is the pattern of life our society regards as normal? With its individualism, its goal of independence from others, its career orientation, its pursuit of wealth, its rootless mobility, its feverish chasing after diversion and entertainment—do we really expect that such a life will be able to bear up and remain intact under the demands of Jesus?

To deny yourself sounds like death when that word is heard by the isolated individual Christian. In the shared life of congregation, if that life is indeed shared, "deny yourself" also speaks of death; but it is a death with others and for others that leads to new life with and for others.

This is not to say that each Christian must put off struggling to obey Christ until his or her congregation becomes a genuine community. Perhaps the process must occur in reverse: the demands of Jesus can lead us to one another in our struggle to do the truth we perceive. Here is a new grace within the severity of Jesus' demands: that they drive the disciples closer together toward a more literal interdependence; that they strip us of our selves in order that we may find new selves in relation to others; that they take away our merely private lives, enshrouded in self-concern, to draw us into new life together.

The command of Christ, the work of his engendering deed, comes into the world like a stranger, seeking a place of hospitality, creating for itself a home. That place is called Christian community. It is that place where the dignity of the good work as obedience is preserved, where a Christian man or woman can learn the discipline of Jesus Christ.

6

HEARERS
OF THE WORD

We meet together in order to read the sacred texts, if the nature of the times compels us to warn about or recognize anything present. In any case, with the holy words we feed our faith, we arouse our hope, we confirm our confidence.

Tertullian

*T*he autumn of 1982 was a bewildering and painful time for the nation of Israel. The invasion of and withdrawal from Lebanon, the tragedy of civilian suffering and the horror of the Beirut massacres had become history. The nation underwent a period of self-examination, with voices from every sector of society debating what the events of the recent past meant to Israel's identity and self-understanding. Out of a cacophony of accusations and recriminations, charges and counter-charges, came a voice that seemed to speak with the quiet authenticity of an ancient prophet: "We have given up history for the sake of geography."

When that "history" all started, that is, when Abraham in the Ur of the Chaldees heard the Word of God—the call and the promise—he gave up geography for the sake of history. He was set on a pilgrimage that would lead to a people that in turn would lead to a person who would live and die for all people. What unfolded was, in reality, a history of the Word of God until that Word of God would enter history in flesh and blood. It was a history of that faithful Word of God that called forth and created a covenant people, and the history of the covenant people's response to that Word. Whether we speak of the old covenant or the new, Israel or the church—or more accurately speak of them together in an inseparable connectedness—we are speaking of a covenant community that exists only in, by, and through the Word of God. No other description, analysis, or event is an adequate explanation of the Judeo-Christian faith and the social realities that are the expression of that faith.

The church in its most local and fundamental unit, the Christian congregation, exists, insofar as it is the church of Jesus Christ, in response to the Word of God. The Word is the source of its life. Without the Word of God the church, like the world, is without form and void. It is a body without a heart, a voice without a message, and eyes without sight. It may well exist as a social organization, a religious institution, or a tax-exempt corporation, but it will not exist as the church of Jesus Christ. It will have given up its history for the sake of its cultural geography. As an organization it may function as a convenient social expression of national values, an entertainment center to occupy the time of the young, a meeting point for various and sundry clubs; it may offer the nostrums of pop-psychology and the analyses of contemporary quasi-sociology. But unless it is a community of faith whose life is centered in the ever present hearing of the Word of God, it is something less than the covenant people of God. All expressions of what the church is that do not find their beginning and their ending in the Word of God are inauthentic expressions, giving up not only our history but our identity as well, for our Christian identity is inseparably tied to our self-understanding. And the Christian community's self-understanding in light of the Word of God is indissolubly tied to the cross. Christian understanding is quite literally a standing under the cross.

The crisis of faith and faithfulness within our Christian congregations should, at least partially, be understood as a crisis of the silence of the Word of God. We have not continued in God's Word, either as hearers or doers. We have sought our nourishment in that which was never intended to be our sustenance, our renewal from sources that in themselves are not the words of life, and our direction from myriad contemporary voices that have not yet heard the first word of the Christian journey, "Follow me." Paul's words to the Romans concerning his Jewish brothers and sisters are an important reminder to us in our current dilemma: "Faith comes from what is heard and what is heard comes by the preaching of Christ" (Rom. 10:17).

Our purpose in this chapter is to suggest the importance of the centrality of the Scriptures to the life of the congregation, and to seek for ways in which they might once again become authoritative, informative, and transformative. A new grasp of the authoritative function of Scripture does not imply a new bibliolatry, a louder shouting of Scripture, or more Bible "quotations" in the contemporary practice of preaching. Rather, we are concerned that the Christian congregation once again become a covenant community constituted by being hearers of the Word—a community of people who live their story because they know their story.

A HEARTH OF REFLECTION

Becoming hearers of the Word begins well before we open the pages of the Bible. It calls for a renewal of our humanity at the most fundamental level, for it demands the transformation of our capacity to listen and to speak. As Rabbi Abraham Heschel has said,

The renewal of man involves a renewal of language. To the man of our age, nothing is as familiar and trite as words. Of all things they are the cheapest, most abused, and least esteemed. They are the objects of perpetual defilement. We all live in them, but since we fail to uphold their independent dignity, they turn waif, elusive—a mouthful of dust. When placed before the Bible, the words of which are like dwellings made of rock, we do not know how to find the door. There is no understanding of the God of Israel without deep sensitivity to the holiness in words. For what is the Bible? Holiness in words. And we destroy all the gates of the Bible

by the ongoing desecration of the power of the word. . . . Prom-
iscuity of expression, loss of sensitivity to words, has nearly destroyed the fortress of the spirit. And the fortress of the spirit is
the *debar*, the word. Words have become slums. What we need is
a renewal of words.[1]

The biblical message remains incomprehensible if it is not heard
within a context of essential human attitudes and sensitivities.

The tyranny of thoughtlessness. As a community committed
to "holiness in words" the Christian congregation is called to be
a hearth of reflection. By reflection we mean simply the reverent
consideration of life, the passion to see life in its wholeness, its
wonder and mystery under God. We mean the nourishment of the
reverent intelligence, the conscious cultivation of that particularly human capacity the Bible calls the *heart*.

Secularization happens inside us as well as all around us. We
are pointing here to the secularization of consciousness on a mass
level. This may be described as a virtual shrinking of the vision of
reality in the minds of men and women around us, and in our own
minds as well. Words themselves become small: "life" comes to
be defined as mere existence; "happiness" comes to mean mere
satisfaction. The intelligence and imagination are riveted to the
earth. Kierkegaard, a century ago, discerned a growing thoughtlessness and clearly understood that such a diminishing of mind
would make a person something less than human.

> As everywhere ingenuity and business increase, there comes to
> be in every generation more and more men who toilsomely labor
> throughout their whole life far down in the deep subterranean re-
> gions; aye, like miners, who never see the light of day, so these
> unfortunates never come to see the light; those elevating, simple,
> primary thoughts about how glorious it is to be human.[2]

---

[1]Abraham Heschel, "The Jewish Notion of God," in *Theology of Renewal*, ed. L. K. Shook, 2 vols. (New York: Herder and Herder, 1968)
1:115.

[2]Søren Kierkegaard, *Edifying Discourses: A Selection*, ed. Paul L.
Holmer, trans. D. F. Swenson and L. M. Swenson (New York: Harper and
Row, Harper Torchbooks, 1958) 238.

Thoughtlessness and failure of imagination are not usually included in the list of cardinal sins. But if "those elevating, simple, primary thoughts" are forgotten, our quality of life is deeply altered. To take one example, if we are becoming a less compassionate society, it surely has to do with the inability to participate imaginatively in another's suffering. When the mind and imagination are focused on the ground right in front of you, the suffering of another has no compelling reality; it makes no reflective hold on you.

What is tragic from a specifically Christian perspective is that, in the collective collapse of reflection, the hearts of women and men can no longer contain the desires, aspirations, passions, even the questions, that the Christian gospel addresses. Jesus said, "Blessed are those who hunger and thirst after righteousness." But we seem to have become a society of people for whom that word *righteousness* evokes not even the lightest of passions.

We need to glimpse some of the forces that have brought us to this point. It is essential to recognize that thoughtlessness is being cultivated almost systematically. Mindlessness has become a determining structure all about us.

We may begin with the obvious, the *edifice of advertising* around us. More is spent on advertising in the United States in a given year than is spent on all educational institutions and all religious institutions combined! It is hardly an oversimplification to name as the sole object of this advertising the focus of our imaginations upon the banal and immediate, the shallow world of satisfaction-dissatisfaction. It creates and inflates insatiable needs. In the bluntest terms, advertising is the artful cultivation of what Christianity has always called greed and covetousness.

Advertising is, of course, only one of the grosser sides of an incredibly diffuse presence of the mass media in our lives. A mere seventy years ago, almost every word a person heard was uttered by a human face from not more than a few feet away. Today, words form an overarching, almost mystical presence around us. Some years ago, Richard Hoggart, in his book *The Uses of Literacy*, reviewed much of the "popular media" to discern some of its effects especially on working class families in England. The media, he believes, trivialize the familiar and elevated concepts by which we normally evaluate life: "progress is conceived as a seeking material possessions, equality as a moral leveling and freedom as a ground for irresponsible pleasure." Moreover, through the creation of a vicarious, spectators' world, the possibility of a genuine response to real life gradually dries up. There disappears from life "the sense of tension in living and with it any real taste for its challenges."[3]

Less obvious in the collective collapse of reflection is the effect of an increasingly *technical environment* on our thought and imagination. By a technical environment we mean simply that our lives are given over in large part to the use of techniques, most of which we do not understand, but which we must nevertheless employ to get what we want. We will not for a moment argue that technical progress is somehow inherently evil. Yet progress among a sinful race is inevitably ambiguous, and it is worth trying to discern why.

It is sobering to contemplate how thoroughly our lives are given over to procedures someone has devised to allow us to get efficiently what we want when we want it. Can we be so innocent (or so obtuse) as to suspect that such a way of life, entirely different from the way previous societies have lived, will not have far-reaching effects on us spiritually? We should be put immediately on our guard when we remember that technique is essentially a way of achieving and maintaining power over our surroundings. And power (control and manipulation) in the New Testament is always linked to temptation. Clearly, one of the temptations inherent in technique is the illusion of self-autonomy. If one can seemingly always work the world at will, what becomes of that creaturely sense of limitation so vital to the worship of God?

The most frightful effect of the rule of technique is that the one whose life is given over to techniques may come to regard life itself as a technique. So one becomes impatient and suspicious of those needs and experiences that are not subject to manipulation

---

[3]Richard Hoggart, *The Uses of Literacy* (London: Chatto and Windus, 1957) 163, 277.

and control. That is, one becomes impatient with all that is mysterious or wonderful, with whatever cannot be immediately grasped. Yet all that is finally worthy of our attention, all that has to do with the dimension of morality and spirituality, is characterized by mystery and wonder.[4]

There is indeed a great deal of impatience with mystery in our churches. One hears Christians speak about prayer as if it were some sort of ultimate technique for securing what one cannot obtain with lesser techniques. Certainly without a sense of mystery one is entirely unable to comprehend the character and power of evil. In a world governed by technique, evil is simply a flaw that can be repaired with greater knowledge and the more perfect application of procedure. There is no remembrance of a darkness in the heart, beyond all explanation, that exults in destruction.

Quite simply, a mind without a sense of mystery is a mind with no room for reflection and wisdom. It will be simply assumed that whatever can be controlled ought to be. The question of the justice or the wisdom of it will not be tolerated. In the world of technique, one is never challenged to be a thoughtful, imaginative human being; it is quite enough simply to function as an intelligent control center.

Finally, a life without a sense of its own mystery is subhuman and becomes intolerable. With our techniques we may achieve a kind of generalized comfort, but such comfort is empty of meaning.

The cognitive effects of greed. What gives rise to the *willingness* to surrender ourselves to mindlessness? Such willingness is closely connected to what the Bible calls greed, envy, and covetousness. We all recognize these states of mind as evil. But the particular concern here is what Peter Berger has called the cognitive effects of greed, the part that greed plays in the way one perceives the world. E. F. Schumacher, the late British economist and phi-

---

[4]In our understanding of mystery and its relation to our technical environment and the decline of wisdom, we have been guided by the French philosopher, Gabriel Marcel, in his *Mystery of Being*, trans. G. S. Fraser, 2 vols. (South Bend IN: Gateway Editions, 1977).

losopher, wrote with clarity and frankness about the absence of wisdom in the economic life of the West: "the cultivation and expansion of needs is the antithesis of wisdom." About greed specifically he wrote:

> If human vices such as greed and envy are systematically cultivated, the inevitable result is nothing less than a *collapse of intelligence*. A man driven by greed or envy loses the power of seeing things as they really are, of seeing things in their roundness and wholeness, and his very successes become failures. If whole societies become infected by these vices, they may indeed achieve astonishing things but they become increasingly incapable of solving the most elementary problems of everyday existence.[5]

That greed is indeed "systematically cultivated" in our way of life hardly needs demonstration, although an in-depth analysis of the effects of greed in the common life would be useful, if depressing. For now, it is enough to point to the double-edged truth: if we are to restore reflection to its place in the ordering of our lives, then we must rise above greed; and if we are to rise above greed, we must find the strength for critical reflection about our experience.

We have spoken of the relevance of the New Testament themes of the principalities and powers to the understanding of our urban environment. There are structures of evil that take on an omnipresence, that in a given time and place achieve a momentum of their own and enslave human beings body and soul. In light of this understanding of evil, we are able to recognize the structure of thoughtlessness—in its direct hostility to the knowledge and love of God—as among these present principalities and powers.

> Where is the Life we have lost in living?
> Where is the wisdom we have lost in knowledge?
> Where is the knowledge we have lost in information?
> ....
> Endless invention, endless experiment,

---

[5]E. F. Schumacher, *Small is Beautiful* (New York: Harper and Row Perennial Library, 1973) 31.

Brings knowledge of motion, but not of stillness;
Knowledge of Speech, but not of Silence,
Knowledge of words, and ignorance of the Word.[6]

The renewal of reflection. In a world of shrunken realities, largeness of mind becomes a Christian virtue. It must be a mark of the church's identity to demonstrate her freedom from the tyranny of thoughtlessness. Christian communities, however small, must find the resources to keep the fires of reflection burning.

In one sense, this is a defensive need, so that faith can survive in our own hearts and the hearts of our children. When the Jewish people found themselves in Babylon and were called upon to sing the Lord's song in the strange land, their response was the formation of the synagogue—a place of learning, reflection, study, and discernment in the light of faith and worship. Similarly, the congregation must recognize its place in maintaining what the sociologists call a "cognitive minority." Our Christian knowledge has come to be a deviant knowledge, a knowledge not socially shared. Such knowledge is imperiled, not only in its confrontation with the "outside," but, more importantly, within our own heads and hearts. The status of the cognitive minority is invariably one of tension and challenge.

Yet the Christian minority must forgo all attempts to maintain itself by its own propaganda that counters the propaganda of mass culture. Religious propaganda—the attempt to force opinion and loyalty by short-cut, oversimplified, and false but useful versions of "truth"—can only disillusion and destroy faith in the long run. What we must seek in our common life is the exorcism of the very spirit of propaganda by the passion and reverence for truth.

For the Christian congregation the first focus for reflection is always the Bible. But it will not do simply to read in search of the right religious "information." What we seek is a vision of life and of God that is whole, that can contain the wide range of life's ambiguities, and that can sustain us in the concrete dilemmas we face.

---

[6]T. S. Eliot, "Choruses from the Rock," in *The Complete Poems and Plays, 1909-1950* (New York: Harcourt, Brace and World, 1962) 96.

The place of Christian reflection is to elucidate and articulate a vision that has the power and the beauty to lift the mind and imagination above the oppressive "everydayness" of the secular world. Such a lifting of the mind does not create faith, for only God, finally, can grant faith. Yet reflection can help to maintain that zone of freedom in the heart into which God may move. Nor does a cumulative lifting of minds create a congregation that is a company of intellectuals. We are not concerned with "intellect" as measured by "I.Q." examinations. But there is an enlarging of vision that is consummate with Christian faith, that is open to the mystery of life and therefore ready to learn. Such a quality of heart one ought to be able to learn among the followers of the one who said, "the truth shall make you free."

We said this need for reflection is in part defensive; it is certainly more than that. For in a world empty of reflection, one of the most precious gifts the church can offer the world is a clear sight and a pondering heart. This is not everything. Sophia is not pistis; wisdom is not faith. But faith assumes the inquiring heart. Where no truth is reverenced, how will the Truth be discerned?

THE PREACHING/TEACHING MINISTRY

For the nourishing of this wisdom and the proclamation of this truth, the church demands a deepening of the teaching and preaching ministry in our common life. There must be those whose vocation it is to clarify our minds as well as warm our hearts, who can open to us all the gates of the Scriptures. Singing the Lord's song demands that we know the words as well as the music. For this reason the preaching/teaching ministries were central to the gifts Christ gave to the church: "that some should be apostles, some prophets, some evangelists, some pastors and teachers to equip the saints for the work of ministry, for building up the body of Christ" (Eph. 4:11-12).

Preaching and teaching, Bible study and catechism, theological reflection and application are indispensable to the faith, renewal, identity, and action of the Christian congregation. For the church to "be church" each person within the body of Christ should be trained to assume his or her function within the "priesthood of all believers." This is not to be understood as a negative, anticlerical slogan. Rather, the biblically and theologically trained, called, ordained, and committed minister is vital to the practice of the priesthood of believers. What is needed, however, is an adequate understanding and practice by both clergy and laity of the purpose and function of such a ministry within the life of the congregation.[7]

The minister is too often perceived as a jack or jill of all trades. He or she does not "do" the work of the church. The teaching minister's function, as we have seen from Ephesians, is to equip the saints for the work of ministry. The minister is above all else a servant of the Word of God. The minister is a preacher/teacher/ theologian within the covenant community. He or she is what Langdon Gilkey has called a one-person seminary.[8] Administration, public relations, fund raising, and a host of other ministerial "job descriptions" and expectations are not the primary domain of the ordained minister. On the other hand, the "priesthood of all believers" should never become an excuse for the absence of the trained minister/theologian. It will take both clergy and laity working together for the local congregation to become hearers of the Word. We are in desperate need of a trained clergy who will again become servants of the Word and a laity who will not only understand that but expect it. When the minister of the church is no longer a servant of the Word, the laity of the church will no longer be prepared, informed, and trained as a priesthood in the world. The absence of the Word leads to an ignorance of the faith. A church ignorant of its faith and how that faith functions in and answers to the contemporary world cannot possibly maintain its Christian identity.

What the church brings to the world in the first instance and in the final analysis is the Word of Christ. The church can never be a better source of entertainment, psychological insight, or sociological analysis than the contemporary world around it whose

---

[7]See above, chap. 4.

[8]Langdon Gilkey, How the Church Can Minister to the World without Losing Itself (New York: Harper and Row, 1964) 98.

business and purpose it is to provide expertise in their own fields. The integrity of the church depends on the integrity with which it preserves the ministry of the Word.

The responsibility for this inevitably falls on the trained preacher/teacher/theologian within the community. One of the tragedies of modern Protestantism is that to a wide degree our pulpits are filled with ministers who no longer conceive of their primary identity as being servants of the Word. There is somehow a felt need to legitimize and validate one's ministry by acquiring training or expertise in some other more "respected" or "recognized" field of endeavor. The problem is only exacerbated by a laity who want their ministers to be slick and appealing "fronts" for their congregation with the ability to sound nice for twenty minutes on a Sunday morning. Thus the minister is expected to function as administrator and public relations person throughout the week and pleasant but inoffensive entertainer on the Lord's Day. It is no wonder that, as Paul Scherer reports, "A Roman Catholic author is on record as having expressed the opinion that if ever Protestantism should be found dead of an assassin's wound, the dagger in its back would be the Protestant sermon."[9]

There is no way to overcome this dilemma until the Christian minister goes back into the study before he or she climbs into the pulpit. If the minister's existence is not a theological existence the congregation that is served will live in a theological vacuum. If the Word is not broken in the minister's heart through the week it cannot possibly be shared in the community's life on Sunday. If the church's history and theological struggles and formulations do not continually inform the minister's thinking, they will never become a part of the subsoil that will give depth and nourishment to the congregation's identity, worship, and mission. If the minister has not paid careful attention to the cries and whispers of the people, listening through the stethoscope of the Christian gospel, the divine word and the human word will never meet in the clar-

---

[9]Paul Scherer, The Word God Sent (Grand Rapids MI: Baker Book House, 1965) 3.

ifying, judging, and redeeming event that is to be Christian preaching.

Preaching is never simply a divine word or simply a human word. Like the Incarnation, it is a divine word in the human word. The preacher's task is to keep the Word and the world together on behalf of the congregation. This occurs not from a position of religious infallibility, moral superiority, or spiritual perfection but from a life that is lived in openness to both the Word and the world. Preaching is not, therefore, a matter of imparting information of historical or theological interest. To be sure, it deals with the historical and the theological but not in isolation from the lived experience of the congregation. Christ is present again to the world in the preaching event. Likewise, the world around us and in us is made present to Christ in the preaching event. The failure of either of these dynamics is a failure in being preachers and hearers of the Word.

The much vaunted value of relevance in Christian preaching is also much misunderstood. Relevance has as much to do with the biblical story as it does with the contemporary world. At the same time, the insistence on biblical preaching has as much to do with the contemporary world as it does with the Scriptures. The preacher who weaves together random thoughts on the week's news headlines, the recently published book, or the latest article from the denominational publication may not be the slightest bit relevant; the minister who laces every second thought in the sermon with a Bible quotation is not necessarily biblical. "Only authentically biblical preaching can be really relevant; only vitally relevant preaching can be really biblical."[10]

Biblical and relevant preaching occurs when the central story and overarching themes of the scriptural narrative become a part of the ongoing experience of the congregation's life. It is not simply a matter of knowing about something that happened "back then." Nor is it a matter of knowing facts, stories, names, places, and events—as if a knowledge of the Bible's contents leads auto-

---

[10]John Knox, The Integrity of Preaching (Nashville: Abingdon Press, 1957) 27.

matically to knowledge of God. The knowledge of God, the *da'ath elohim* of the Old Testament without which the covenant people are destroyed, is not intellectual understanding but passionate involvement with the God who is the subject of the story of the ongoing relationship with a God-chosen people in a God-created world. In Christian preaching the biblical story, truth, and vision of life become an ongoing story, a judging and redemptive truth, and a way of seeing for the individual Christian and the congregation in the contemporary society. God continues to judge, call, promise, and redeem through the divine Word made manifest in the preaching event. Biblical narrative becomes living history in the shaping of the life of the Christian community. Biblical preaching will take us back into history and thrust us out into history in a living covenant relationship with God. All of the pain, peace, hope, despair, frustration, beauty, confusions, strivings, absurdities, and meaning of our humanity will find their place alongside of and be informed by the humanity that is the object of God's concern in the Bible. In the preaching event that is both biblical and relevant the Christian congregation forms its self-understanding, interprets its words, and shapes its life according to the gospel it confesses. Failure at this point will inevitably erode the inner life of the congregation as an authentic Christian community and the external witness of the congregation as bearers of the Word of Christ to the world.

THEOLOGICAL MEDIATION

But more is required of the Christian congregation as hearers of the Word than a minister who functions as a servant of the Word. That is simply the essential foundation and starting point for the whole community to be servants of the Word. In order for that Word to become flesh again, to become embodied in Christian living and Christian action, it must become a part of the understanding and life of the members of the congregation. Not only is the world of the Bible brought to the people but the people themselves bring a world to the Bible. Making sense out of the collision of those two worlds is a formidable task that can only be accomplished by the people and the preacher working together.

There is often a terrible gap for both the minister and the people between the work-a-day modern world of science, technology, business, and leisure and the world of the Bible, theology, and Christian ethics. It is as if neither world can stand the scrutiny of the other. The unfortunate reality is that there is often an unacknowledged acceptance of this gap as if that is simply the way it must be, and so the Christian lives schizophrenically—there is one reality for the nine-to-five world and another reality for the Sunday school and worship hour.

Yet there is only one world that is the object of God's love. Overcoming the disconnectedness is the task of the congregation as hearers of the Word. Dialogue between preacher and people is a *way of life* for the Christian congregation. The preaching event *and* theological education of the congregation must go hand in hand. The classical definition of theology is "faith in search of understanding." It is crucial for the community's theologian/minister and modern lay people to engage in this search together. Otherwise faith will be aligned with the past and understanding with the future. Theology, therefore, could as easily be defined today as understanding in search of faith. The modern dimensions of life and thought need not, indeed should not, be left behind at the door of the sanctuary. Theological education within the congregation is not a matter of passing on unexamined dogmas of a previous generation. It is a wrestling together in community with any and every question we face with the best we can bring to the task from Scripture, tradition, reason, and experience. Through such endeavors faith becomes a living reality in which our understandings are reformulated, tested, and often altered, for faith is more a process one lives than a possession one has or protects. The theological enterprise carried on at the congregational level can thus be an extremely liberating influence for a faith we once were afraid to question, a doctrine we secretly felt was hopelessly outdated and unrelated to life, and a contemporary world view that may have been technically wide but humanly shallow. The goal toward which our congregations need to move as hearers of the Word is a clergy whose function is that of preacher/theologian for the sake of the community and a theologically informed laity whose function is that of priests in the world.

LIVING CONNECTIONS

As hearers of the Word the community is an ellipse that moves about the pulpit and the lectern (preaching and theology) seeking living connections between the Word proclaimed in the congregation and the shape of the life of the congregation lived in the world. At least four connections should be sought in the preaching event and theological reflection.

The pastoral connection. The pastoral connection is that point where the Christian gospel nourishes the life of the follower of Christ. It is food for the soul and sustenance for the journey. Wounds in our existence are tended by the healing Word of Christ. The pastoral connection is where preaching is encouragement in the clearest possible way for the life of faith lived in a world of deep contradictions and practical difficulties. The problems and questions of fear, failure, sin, anxiety, unbelief, and suffering at the most personal level should be addressed in Christian preaching. The issues discussed in the chapter on pastoral care become the universe of kerygmatic discourse. Our emptiness and our fullness, our joy and our sorrow, our dreams and our nightmares are taken up into the gospel story when preaching makes the pastoral connections. Without this feeding, nourishing, healing, encouraging, public word for the hungry, anguished, confused, and wasted places in our private lives, faith will never function in a transforming way.

The prophetic connections. Dietrich Bonhoeffer once told his students at the underground seminary in Finkenwalde that every sermon should contain a little heresy. This was spoken at a time when the prevailing orthodoxy practiced by the German church was drawn more from the Ministry for Ecclesiastical Affairs in the government of the Third Reich than from the gospel of Christ. The preaching of the Word in this context of cultural or national orthodoxy would indeed appear to be heresy.

The problem of preaching the Word of God (which will often clash with the prevailing orthodoxy of cultural religion) is, of course, much older than 1943. Its history stretches from the eighth-century prophets of Israel through the life of Jesus and on down to the present day. But the prophetic connection is often avoided or ignored because of the tension it creates within the congregation or between the congregation and the society in which it must live. The end result is a cultural captivity of the Word of God—a kind of domestication that tames it for our own ideological purposes.

The prophetic word challenges our tendency toward idolatry, our comfortable refuge in our various parochialisms, and our apathy toward justice. In prophetic preaching we are confronted not just with the personal dimension but with the social dimension of life as well. Structural evil in such issues as race, poverty, war, and the inequities and injustices in the economic order are seen in light of the righteousness (justice) of God. The fact that these are massive and complicated structural problems, and the fact that as individuals we inevitably participate in these structures, does not mean they should be ignored in Christian preaching. We may not be wholly guilty, but neither are we completely innocent.

The prophetic connection should be made in preaching not because the minister is a self-appointed prophet who enjoys berating people and gives the impression that he or she is exempt, but because he or she is a servant of the Word who feels the guilt and bears the pain of the prophetic utterance. Prophetic connections in preaching are not brow-beating fulminations broadcast indiscriminately into the air with no regard for the complexity of social evil and our relationship to it. But prophetic connections *are connections*. Arising from the prophetic word itself, such preaching will call us to shared responsibility, corporate confession, and genuine repentance; to specific ways we can work toward justice; and finally, to a recognition that, while only God can usher in the kingdom of God, we can live lives more consonant with the kingdom's values as we watch and pray for its coming.

In the meantime the congregation should have the courage to say to itself and its society, "In the name of Jesus Christ certain things should or should not be acceptable. The kingdom is at hand. Repent and believe the good news." Our faithfulness to the Lordship of Christ is probably threatened more by our idolatry in a thoroughgoing cultural Christianity than by anything else. Only prophetic connections in the preaching event can continue to shake us loose from the demigods that claim our loyalty, affection, and worship.

The liturgical connections. By liturgical connections we simply mean that preaching is both a part of worship and worship itself, pointing to the centrality of the sacrament of the Word along with the sacrament of the Lord's Supper. The Word of God is present in both preaching and Eucharist. Just as communion is more than remembering the past event as we share in the presence of Christ through bread and wine, preaching is more than retelling an ancient story. In preaching, the gospel itself is present and we are participating in the judging and redemptive power of God who continues to act in and through the gospel. Just as ancient Israel participated in the Exodus experience through the liturgical formulations of retelling and recreating the story in their common worship (Deut. 26:5-11), so does the church participate in the acts of God in Christ in the preaching of the gospel. The liturgical connection in preaching is what keeps preaching from being mere exegesis of an ancient text. The congregation does more than "commute" back to the world of the Bible for religious, doctrinal, or moral instruction during a sermon on a Sunday morning. They participate in the events of their faith through the presence of the living Word.

When preaching is understood not only as proclamation *of* but also as participation *in* the story of God and God's people, then it becomes increasingly clear that the fullness of that story must be present within the congregation during the course of the year. The liturgy and the lectionary go hand in hand to take us up into that story. The set lectionary readings anchor preaching to the central biblical themes rather than to the limited "favorites" of any given preacher. By using the lectionary the congregation is also assured of the overall sense of the story as it unfolds in history. That in itself can be a powerful force in shaping the congregation's sense of attachment to and continuing participation in the ongoing history. The purpose of biblical preaching by means of the lectionary is to enable us not simply to see the text but to see through the text into our own lives and culture with a clarifying vision of faith.

The theological connections. Preaching the gospel is never simply transmission of a text. It is always a translation into the thought world of those who bring their questions and struggles to the Bible. These two worlds are both radically different and remarkably the same. For the church to be both biblical and relevant these two worlds must be brought together. Theological mediation is the only possible way this can be done.

What do we mean by theological mediation or connections? In its most basic form, the church "does theology" when it asks how the biblical story and the truth claims of that story function in light of modern knowledge, thought forms, and experience. We do theology when we ask what we believe, how we believe it, why we believe it, and what difference it makes that we believe it. We do theology when we ask how the church signifies the biblical story in the contemporary world. We do theology when we seek to understand the meaning and function of the central doctrines of the Christian faith for shaping the identity and action of the church. We do theology when we ask questions of the Bible and the theological tradition and when we allow the Bible and the tradition to ask their own questions of us. We do Christian theology when we ask who Jesus Christ is for us today and who we are because of Jesus Christ. There is an urgency for this task to be done at the congregational level if we are to have a church composed of people who are both thoughtful and believing. Without theological mediation of the faith we confess and the truth we believe, the church will be left adrift in mediocrity at best and be defenseless at worst.

The Christian community learns from Jesus of Nazareth to make its dwelling in that "fortress of the spirit" that is the Word of God. The one whom we confess to be the Word of God incarnate encountered the adversary with the word of Scripture (Matt. 4:4). In his ministry he preached the word of Scripture (Luke 4:16ff.). In his dying he prayed the word of Scripture (Matt. 27:46). And in his resurrection he interpreted to his disciples the word of Scripture (Luke 24:27). To this ancient word of Scripture, the living Christ adds his authoritative voice: "If you continue in my word you are truly my disciples" (John 8:31).

7

A TABLE
FELLOWSHIP

Agape is truly heavenly food. . . . The meal occurs because of love . . . which is a proof of a generous and shared good will. . . . The one who eats of this meal shall obtain the best of the things which pertain to reality, the kingdom of God, since this one has had a care here for the holy assembly of love. . . . Love is not a meal, but let the banquet depend on love.

Clement of Alexandria

Sometime during the Second World War a phrase came into use that might serve as a caption for the history of our century: "the displaced person." The list of peoples who in our lifetime have been forced to flee their homes goes on and on—East Germans, Czechs, Pakistanis, Cambodians, Vietnamese, Angolans, Lebanese, Nicaraguans, Guatemalans; and among ethnic and religious groups—Jews, Muslims, Hindus, Christians, and others.

Many others have looked on this ceaseless flow of homeless peoples. Our heart goes out to them in the unspeakable hardship of their plight. Their homelessness also tells a true and haunting story about our common human predicament. For many of us the term "refugee" has taken on great metaphorical weight. In the first place, mobility is a chief requirement for our highly individualized way of life, making the cultivation of friendship and real involvement with others very difficult. But there is also that inner displacement experienced by the person who no longer feels "at home" with his or her own personal history—cut off from familiar ideas, familiar religions, and familiar interpretations of life.

Christians sometimes lament that we have become a society of unbelievers, while failing to look down into what one might call the "basement of unbelief." That is, for many, the bottom has fallen out of life. What they disbelieve is nothing so certain as God. What they disbelieve is life itself, life's dependability, life's goodness. Such skepticism is not easily verbalized, but it festers in the bottom of the heart and hollows out a chasm of loneliness.

The phrase "displaced person" describes our existence through yet another dimension. In a short story by that title Flannery O'Connor tells the tale of a Polish refugee who is brought by a priest to live and work on a farm in the Southern United States. He is the sojourner, the stranger who cannot even speak the language and whose name no one can pronounce. But by a strange reversal that is as true as life, his life and death among the local residents of the farm reveals that they also are displaced persons. When the stranger is crushed by the wheel of a tractor, Mrs. McIntyre, the farm owner, "was too shocked by the experience to be quite herself. Her mind was not taking hold of all that was happening. She felt she was in some foreign country where the people bent over the body were natives, and she watched like a stranger while the dead man was carried away in the ambulance." In the end, her health is broken and she is confined to her bed. "Not many people remembered to come out to the country to see her except the old priest. He . . . would come in and sit by the side of her bed and explain the doctrines of the Church."[1]

---

[1]Flannery O'Connor, "The Displaced Person," in The Complete Stories (New York: Farrar, Straus and Giroux, 1971) 235.

There is no doubt that in our urban environment many people feel the weight of being "strangers and sojourners," either literally or metaphorically. But from the beginning, Christians grasped hold of the image of the stranger and sojourner. Their experience with suffering and death taught them to regard all earthly life under all conditions as a perilous pilgrimage. But more, this image had for them a paradoxical joy. For in Christ the eternal God had come to tabernacle for awhile with them, to make the perilous journey; and he knew the way through the wilderness. Jesus said, as he faced death, "I go to prepare a place for you," and Christians knew that "place" was nothing less than the presence of God. The father of the faithful was a nomad, and all his children bear his image, "having acknowledged that they were strangers and sojourners on the earth" (Heb. 11:13).

Among nomads and pilgrims hospitality is elevated to a sacred duty and a saving grace. Surely this is why in the Christian Scriptures the act of hospitality and the table of fellowship are held sacred. These acts become the occasion and the symbol for the expression of our life with God. When Paul wrote to the Roman Christians, "Welcome one another as Christ has welcomed you" (Rom. 15:7), he was invoking the power of that symbol to sum up the meaning of the common life in Christ. The centrality of hospitality and table fellowship becomes obvious when we begin to take seriously the fact that, after all, at the center of the life of the church there is the meal. If we are to be truly a human church we need urgently to grasp that this meal, the Lord's Supper, while it is our most sacred act, is also our most simply human act.

In this chapter we will explore the meaning of the Christian eucharistic meal for the life of the congregation. We want to ask how it is that this central Christian sacrament can in fact *sacramentalize our daily life together*, our receiving of the stranger in our midst, and all our occasions of hospitality as we "break bread from house to house."

HOSPITALITY

When Christians break the bread in communion with their Lord, they invoke the action and the words of Jesus who, on the night of his betrayal, took bread, blessed and broke it, and said, "This do in remembrance of me." But to understand the eucharistic meal as simply springing spontaneously from the words of Jesus is to miss the depth and meaning of his Supper. The sacred meals of the first Christians were new; they bore a new mystery hidden in Christ's words, "This is my body and blood." But these meals also had a lineage almost timeless in its antiquity and limitless in the richness of its associations.

The immediate context of the Lord's Supper was probably a Passover meal. That fact alone is often ignored by Christians. But for those first disciples the Lord's Supper was woven in an intricate web of meanings that brought together the fact of Jesus' "eating and drinking with sinners," his last Passover meal, and especially his "Easter meals" recorded in Luke 24 and John 21. Behind this history of table fellowship with Jesus stretched a long history of the fellowship meal that takes us all the way back to father Abraham when he unwittingly shared hospitality with Yahweh, who "appeared to him by the Oaks of Mamre as he sat at the door of his tent in the heat of the day" (Gen. 18:1-16). It was in the practice of hospitality that he received such an unexpected blessing—the announcement that he and Sarah were to have a son.

The honored status of the stranger was secured by Israel's law, which lifted the act of hospitality to a sacred obligation in response to the love of Yahweh. This concern is not peripheral or secondary, but appears at the center of the Old Testament law tradition.

> For the Lord your God is God of gods and Lord of lords, the great, the mighty, and the terrible God, who is not partial and takes no bribe. He executes justice for the fatherless and the widow, and loves the sojourner, giving him food and clothing. Love the sojourner, therefore; for you were sojourners in the land of Egypt (Deut. 10:17-19).

This passage stands as a climax to the great sermon of Moses as the nation is about to take possession of the land God has given them. These words ground the obligation of hospitality in the great act of God and in Israel's own history as a sojourner in the land of Egypt.

In an ongoing reflection of both Abraham's experience and the sacred obligation of hospitality enshrined in the Torah, Jewish piety understood the stranger as a kind of living sacrament. Of course not every stranger was a messenger from God. But every stranger was the "guest of God." As the Jewish Christian author of the Epistle to the Hebrews admonished his congregation, "Do not neglect to show hospitality to strangers, for thereby some have entertained angels unawares" (Heb. 13:2). With the practice of hospitality and the sharing of the table of fellowship central in the life of Israel and the early church, it should not surprise us that it is at the heart of the ministry of Jesus.

Jesus and table fellowship. The Son of man came eating and drinking. That he did so is not simply an interesting historical fact; it is the gospel. His fellowship at table, his receiving and his being received, had the clearest of meanings for the early Christians. His presence at table had the force of a wordless pronouncement of the presence of God. The table of fellowship became the stage upon which Jesus acted out the drama of God's redemption. More accurately, it became the altar of God's love.

It is a mistake to think that Jesus' practice of table fellowship was in absolute contradiction to the meal piety of the Pharisees. To understand the impact of Jesus' break with the Pharisees it is crucial to realize that many Pharisees at first considered Jesus to be one of their own. He was evidently a holy man in whom the power of God dwelt. He was invited on more than one occasion to the table of the Pharisees and may well have participated on these occasions in the Levitical washings. He shared the deep conviction of every devout Hebrew that the sharing and eating of food was a holy thanksgiving to God.

To the outsider Jesus' band of disciples must have resembled a Pharisaic *Haburah* (a meal-study fellowship common among the Pharisees). We can safely assume that much of his instruction was given to the disciples in the context of a shared meal. Christians naturally focus upon the Last Supper of Jesus, often forgetting that this last meal presupposes many previous meals—meals that would have also included the traditional meal liturgy, beginning with the breaking of bread and ending with the cup of blessing. As Louis Bouyer, one of the great authorities on ancient Jewish and

Christian piety, has written: "all of the meals which [Jesus] had taken with the small group of disciples . . . seem to flow into the preliminaries of the last meal."[2] In that last meal Jesus was not so much "instituting" a new act as he was filling an old and richly symbolic act with new life and meaning.

It was because the piety of Jesus had some resemblance to the Pharisaic piety that his explosion of that piety had such dramatic power. Jesus literally "turns the table" on the Pharisees. The place of hospitality becomes the battle ground where Jesus declares the new initiative of God. "He eats with tax collectors and sinners," they complained. "Why do your disciples not live according to the tradition . . . but eat with hands defiled?" they asked Jesus (Mark 7:5). Though the true Pharisee could not eat without ritually washing hands and garments, Jesus would allow himself to be defiled at the very table of a Pharisee by the touch of the Am-Ha-Ar-etz—the common people, literally, "people of the earth" (Luke 7). Jesus even goes so far as to seek hospitality from Zacchaeus the tax collector.

The force of Jesus' table fellowship with the poor and the sinners was not missed by the early disciples. Where Jesus is present at table, there the true Haburah of God is formed. Where Jesus breaks bread, even the sinners may eat of the life of God. When Jesus is in the house, all the doors to the love of God are left open.

Jesus therefore emerges in the gospel story as the gracious host who welcomes all, even the sinners, to the messianic banquet. It is striking how often in the Gospels Jesus enters the house as a guest, only to assume the role of host. Though the Son of man came into the world as a guest and a stranger with nowhere to lay his head, he feeds the thousands, hosting them in the meal liturgy: "he looked up to heaven, and blessed and broke the loaves . . . and they all ate and were satisfied" (Mark 6:41, 42). When God comes in as guest, he goes out as host.

---

[2]Louis Bouyer, Eucharist, trans. Charles U. Quinn (Notre Dame: University of Notre Dame Press, 1968) 101. See also Joachim Jeremias, The Eucharistic Words of Jesus (New York: Charles Scribner's Sons, 1966).

The Easter meals. In one of the earliest recorded Christian sermons, spoken in the house of Cornelius at Caesarea, Peter proclaimed the resurrection of Christ with these words: "God raised him on the third day and made him manifest . . . to us who were chosen by God as witnesses, *who ate and drank with him after he rose from the dead*" (Acts 10:40, 41). In light of the biblical history of table fellowship perhaps we can glimpse why this fact—that the risen Christ came eating and drinking—was remembered and proclaimed by these early witnesses.

Only the Gospels of Luke and John concern themselves with the circumstances of the resurrection appearances. In both, the fact that the Christ took food with his disciples is remembered in great detail. For the early church it was these "Easter meals" as well as the Last Supper that stood behind the Christian Eucharist.

The appearance of the risen Jesus to the two disciples on the road to Emmaus (Luke 24:13ff.) is a clear foreshadowing of the Christian worship service, in which first the Scriptures are expounded and then the bread is eucharistically blessed, broken, and shared. Having been prepared for the recognition of Christ by the stranger's interpretation of the Scriptures, it is not until the shared meal that "their eyes were opened and they recognized him" (v. 31). The text leaves us perplexed about the nature of this transformation of the disciples' vision. In all the appearances Jesus is both familiar and strangely disguised. But perhaps the moment of recognition lay partly in the sheer familiarity of this act of Jesus. How often had his disciples received the broken bread from their master's hand!

Later in Luke 24 the theme of recognition continues. Now Jesus suddenly appears standing among the gathered disciples. "But they were startled and supposed they saw a spirit" (v. 37). To these frightened disciples Jesus offers two signs of identity: he offers to their sight and touch the marks of his wounds, and he eats with them. The wounds and the eating of the broiled fish serve to confirm his identity to his followers. The Son of man had come eating and drinking with sinners and now comes again even in the glory of resurrection to the same table of fellowship.

Finally, the resurrection meals healed the broken fellowship between Jesus and his followers. The cross had shattered that fellowship, not simply by the separation of death but also by the separation of betrayal. At the moment of his passion all of Jesus' friends had forsaken him. What right have they in his resurrection life? This meaning comes clear in the third recorded Easter meal, the breakfast to which Jesus invited his disciples by the Sea of Tiberias (John 21).

The incident begins with the disciples' return to their old life. It is as if the Jesus story has ended.[3] In the course of their fishing the stranger appears on the shore and directs them in a miraculous catch of fish. This spurs John and Peter to recognition. The others still seem uncertain about the identity of the stranger. They discover that he has built a fire for cooking and they hear his simple invitation: "Come and have breakfast." Then, "none of the disciples dared ask him, 'Who are you?' They knew it was the Lord. Jesus came and took the bread and gave it to them, and so with the fish" (vv. 12-13).

If we recall the implicit meaning of the shared meal to these Hebrews—the sign of brotherhood, of mutual acceptance, of reciprocal worthiness—we cannot miss the silent eloquence of forgiveness. Our impression is confirmed when we hear Jesus, as the meal is ended, ask Peter three times, "Do you love me?" (v. 15). Three times in the courtyard of the high priest Peter had denied his friend and master. Now, having once again broken bread with Jesus, he is granted the painful yet joyful affirmation, "Yes, Lord, you know that I love you" (v. 15).

The risen Christ still comes to be the gracious host of sinners. Almost a century later, an exiled Christian visionary, perhaps the same John who had shared in those first Easter meals, hears the glorified and risen Christ call: "Behold I stand at the door and knock; if any one hears my voice, and opens the door, I will come in to him and eat with him, and he with me" (Rev. 3:20).

----

[3]Even though it is described as the third appearance of Christ, John 21 reads like a first surprise appearance. This has led many scholars to believe the story is perhaps misplaced in the text and is a late addition to the Johannine text.

THE CONGREGATION
AS A TABLE FELLOWSHIP IN CHRIST

The sacred history of hospitality culminates in Jesus Christ. In him God comes to the world as stranger and guest, but also as the gracious host to us who have become strangers to God and to one another. The sacred eucharistic meal of the church is the sacrament of this drama. In our eating and drinking we receive Christ as guest, imploring him, "Stay with us, for night is at hand. . . . Come Lord Jesus!" But in his presence we know he is the true host, welcoming us and establishing fellowship with us sinners. "Blessed are those who come to *his* supper." In this mystery of exchange between host and guests, he opens our eyes, he offers to our sight and touch the marks of his sufferings: "This is my body, take and eat. . . . this is the cup of my suffering, all of you drink of it." In this meal he asks us, "Do you love me?" In this meal he makes of us his holy *Haburah*. Each of us becomes the host to the other, welcoming one another as Christ has welcomed us, greeting one another with the sign of his peace. Around this table we eat and drink of Christ; we eat and drink with Christ. And so we are made into his living body.

But all this does not end as soon as the eucharistic service is concluded. If this meal is the true sign of Christ's gracious presence with us, it has the power to sacramentalize all the daily exchanges of our lives. We go from this holy meal to spread true *eucharistia* and the open hospitality of God in the human community. This is the task of the church of Christ. Every Christian community, no matter how small and powerless, can partake of that mission. Some simple observations arise from what we have learned in a small inner-city Christian community about how such a community can attempt to incarnate the words, "Welcome one another as Christ has welcomed you."

Rules of the open house. In this matter we must first of all become literalists. We cannot imagine being and building a Christian community without each of us being to the other hosts and guests in the simple sense of opening our homes and spreading our tables for one another. This sounds almost too simple to say.

And yet if we seriously attempt to order our lives according to the sacred duty of hospitality, we will discover radical consequences. A home that is open to others must become more focused in its life; it will be open to the scrutiny of others; it will be challenged to become less self-centered and closed off from the world. This vulnerability has obvious risks. There is the possibility that an open house will simply be taken advantage of by selfish or very lonely people.

This brings us to one of the guiding rules of hospitality, the rule of *sharing*. Hospitality ought not to be always the occasion when in our own home we "entertain" guests lavishly. Rather, each one is host and guest, sharing whatever resources we have. If hospitality is frequent, this is very important. Even the very poorest in a community can, and as we have learned, will make offerings in a setting of genuine hospitality. This sort of sharing on the simplest of levels says quite clearly: "We wish no difference to separate us, we must all pull together."

Here a second rule emerges, *simplicity*. If the hospitality we offer is to be a moment of sharing and community-building in which we can partake, then it does not mean the lavish display of the host's resources and skills. Such lavishness often stifles the impulse toward hospitality in others, since they cannot match the display. But simplicity allows all to give and take in the lavish exchange of love. This does not mean our eating and drinking together is somber and graceless. And there are the occasional feasts! But if we are striving for a responsive simplicity, a more just use of our riches, a more participatory community life, then the table of fellowship is a graceful place to learn to do "more with less."

> Simplify and share as a way of identifying with Christ Jesus, born among the poor. . . . You need so little to live, so little to welcome others. When you open your home, too many possessions are a hindrance rather than a help to communion with others.[4]

---

[4]Brother Roger of Taizé, *Parable of Community*, trans. E. Chisholm and the Brothers of Taizé (London: Mowbray, 1980) 80-81.

A third rule of the open house is *diversity and inclusiveness*. Christian hospitality will naturally begin with those in the Christian "family." But of course, even within that family there will be those from whom we feel distant, with whom it appears we have little in common, or whom we simply do not like. Just here hospitality must immediately go to work. How else are we to nourish that sense of community and belonging that so many churches lack?

As the circle of hospitality begins to widen there will be room as well for the "stranger"—for those outside the fellowship of the church. In our experience it is often in this way that a fruitful meeting can take place between non-Christians and the life of the Christian community. After all, the hospitality of Christ reaches across the great chasm that separates us from God. God's invitation travels the whole distance of our alienation. If table fellowship means only the gathering of the same familiar circle of friends, it is hard-pressed to call itself Christian hospitality. But if the door is open to those from whom we have been alienated, then indeed we may claim the friendship of Jesus. To dare to bring strangers together involves risks. Yet, in the inclusive embrace of Christian hospitality there is still the ancient mystery of unexpected blessing—when love links us to those we never knew we could love, when pain and troubles are unearthed and shared, when long-standing hostilities and fears are diffused, when genuine community emerges.

In the first chapter of Mark we are told that at Nazareth Jesus

> entered the house of Simon and Andrew, with James and John. Now Simon's mother-in-law lay sick with a fever, and immediately they told him of her. And he came and took her by the hand and lifted her up, and the fever left her; and she served them.
> That evening, at sundown, they brought to him all who were sick or possessed with demons. And the whole city was gathered together about the door. And he healed many who were sick with various diseases, and cast out many demons (Mark 1:29-34).

Our homes are the symbols of our life, the center of our resources, our sufferings, and our joys. When Christ dwells in the house, his presence brings healing. But if he is there, the door must be open to the others. Each of our houses, our apartments, our rooms, is meant to be that house in Nazareth.

The community at table. Our congregations, in becoming true communities, ought to reclaim the ancient tradition of the common meal, the "Agape." It is encouraging to see that some denominations are now including guidelines, and even liturgies, for such meals.[5] We believe such shared meals can help to recast the life of our churches in the genuine hospitality of the gospel.

All that we have said about sharing and simplicity ought to guide us here as well. Each congregation must find its own way. Here we have an opportunity to bring together our common worship and our simple human sharing. At Disciples House our Sunday celebration of Word and sacrament is followed immediately by one or two hours of sharing simple food provided by someone in the fellowship. We have also found that sometimes holding our congregational planning sessions in the context of hospitality helps us to communicate more openly and to deal more creatively with the tensions that are often necessary to serious discussion.

Along with these regular meals that have become a part of the weekly life of the congregation, there are two special ways the community meal enhances our life and ministry. The first of these emerges naturally enough from celebration of the major Christian "feast-days"—Advent, Christmas, Easter, and Pentecost. Too often these times lack any sense of real festivity in the churches. Some of us with a "low" Protestant heritage have found our faith enriched by a festive marking of time according to the ancient calendar of the church. What better way is there to punctuate the story of Jesus Christ than with such worship meals in which praise and prayer, eating and drinking, game-play and conversing, poetry reading and singing all blend together and rivet our attention to this Christ who comes to eat and drink with sinners? How better can we anticipate the joy of the messianic banquet?

---

[5]See, for example, *The Worship Book,* prepared for use in Presbyterian Churches in the United States (Philadelphia: Westminster Press, 1972) 62.

The reclaiming of festivity is hardly a trivial matter for a people who have been commanded always to "rejoice in the Lord." There is in fact the closest relationship between the capacity to celebrate genuinely the goodness of God and the capacity to live as a genuinely human community. For here all the human gifts are employed in a genuinely "catholic" embrace for the worship of God and the welcoming of the neighbor. Brother Roger of Taizé has often marked this connection between faith, festivity, and the embrace of the world of God.

> If festival disappeared from mankind . . . If we were to wake up one fine morning in a society replete but emptied of all spontaneity . . . If praying became mere words, so secularized that it lost all sense of mystery, leaving no room for the prayer of gesture and posture, for poetry, emotion, or intuition . . . If we were to lose childlike trust in the Eucharist and the Word of God . . . If we were to decline the joy offered by Him who eight times over declares 'Happy' . . . If festival disappears from the Body of Christ, if the Church is a place of retrenchment and not of universal comprehension, in all the world where could we find a place of friendship for the whole of humanity?[6]

The festive meal is the moment par excellence for the church to experience the joy of human fellowship across the generations. Yes, the feasts are for children and allow all of us to be children once again. It is, after all, here in the visible joyous shared life of the community that children learn the Christian way, more than in the most up-to-date and well-equipped church school.

A second way the community meal can prove especially fruitful in the congregation's life is in finding friendship and communication with those who do not share our Christian faith or who are in some way estranged from the church. As we have said, hospitality carries new possibilities in bridging the huge chasm between Christian faith and the secular lives of many men and women.

At Disciples House we have come to call these occasions "open meals." They were inspired simply by the vision of Jesus, who ate

---

[6]Brother Roger, *Parable of Community*, 53-54.

and drank with all sorts of people, and by the realization that when people eat together they end up sharing more than just food. Each month members of our fellowship come together bringing with them some friend or acquaintance, especially those who are not Christian, to spend the evening sharing a simple meal and conversation. Many share the responsibility of the meal. The only caution we observe is trying to ensure that guests are not greatly outnumbered by community members. Such meals, coming regularly each month, give us a chance to invite that person about whom we think, "I wish we had a chance to talk and get to know one another." They allow us to invite the "skipper" off the street, the new immigrant family in the neighborhood, the local Hindu shop keeper with whom we do business. Such times make visible the life of the Christian community.

It is important that these meals have no "purpose," no agenda, except to listen, to try to understand what makes others laugh and cry, what it is from this life they desire. We begin such meals with a simple blessing, and we may say a brief word about our identity as a Christian community, but not many words of explanation are needed. We are often struck by the readiness of people to tell their stories, express their frustrations, and share their hopes. Out of this sometimes strange combination of human beings arise all sorts of encounters—arguments, discussions, counseling sessions; tears, hilarity, anger, and real human warmth. Sometimes genuine friendships have grown up. And some who have come to these meals have later attached themselves in some way to our community in search of an understanding of the Christian faith. But a spirit of recruitment would be deadly to such occasions. There is no claim here to have discovered some "new and effective" technique for carrying out the mission of the church. What we are learning is simply the truth of the ancient link between hospitality and the gospel of Christ.

The Eucharist as a meal. The Lord's Supper is, of course, a sacred meal and the central rite of the church. But if it is to shape our daily life, then the connection between this meal and all our eating and drinking together needs to be recaptured. That is why we believe that *sometimes* the Eucharist ought to be celebrated in the context of a full common meal. In what we are suggesting here, we have not the slightest desire to denigrate the eucharistic liturgies of the churches. Over the last hundred years there has been a great renewal in eucharistic worship and a new recognition that the Lord's Day is incomplete without the Lord's Supper. At last the liturgies of the various denominations are, by a return to the ancient sources, recapturing a unity expressive of the one holy catholic church.[7]

But it is clear from the New Testament and implied by the oldest eucharistic liturgy that for the first Christians the eucharistic meal and the common meal were all of one piece. As in the ancient Jewish meal liturgies, the bread was blessed and broken to begin the meal, representing the supreme food and the common life of the church which is the body of Christ. The cup was passed at the end of the meal. And so the whole table fellowship was sanctified by the presence of Christ.

In the building of a genuinely human Christian community in the midst of our society, nothing is more important than ordering our lives by the act and the implications of the Lord's Supper, the Eucharist. How desperately we need the festival, the embrace of body and mind, the joy in creation, the renewal of friendship, the courage to suffer—all that is given us in this meal. It is our most sacred moment. And it is our most human moment. For what can be more human than eating and drinking together? When so human an act is enjoyed "at the table of the Lord," when Christ himself comes to be our guest and our host, then we are truly the human church in the presence of God.

---

[7]See L. Bouyer's treatment of developments in Protestant and Catholic eucharistic worship in *Eucharist*, 436-74.

8

IN THE FRIENDSHIP OF JESUS

By loving you will be an imitator of God's kindness.
And do not marvel that one is able to be an imitator
of God. One is able if one wills. For happiness is not
in ruling over your neighbors, nor wishing to have
more than the weak, nor being rich and powerful over
those who are in a lower situation. Neither is one able
to imitate God by doing these things; these things are
outside his majesty. But whoever takes upon oneself
the burden of the neighbor . . . is an imitator of God.

Epistle to Diognetus

In the "last discourses" of the Gospel of John we hear Jesus speaking intimately with his small band of disciples.

This is my commandment, that you love one another as I have
loved you. Greater love has no man than this, that a man lay down
his life for his friends. You are my friends if you do what I command you. . . . I have called you friends, for all that I have heard
from my Father I have made known to you. You did not choose
me, but I chose you and appointed you that you should go and

> bear fruit and that your fruit should abide; so whatever you ask
> the Father in my name, he may give it to you. This I command
> you, to love one another (John 15:12-17).

This picture of the Christian community as a circle of friends
called by Jesus, bound together in obedience to him, enjoying the
knowledge of the Father and the certitude of prayer, is certainly
one of the most winsome pictures of the church in the Scriptures.
It is a picture very like the one we discovered in the last chapter.
There the image was the table of fellowship sanctified by the presence of Christ the host. Here the image is the company of friends
laying down their lives for one another in imitation of Jesus.

There is one other passage in the Gospels in which Jesus is
called "friend" and which also recalls our last chapter. "The Son
of man has come eating and drinking; and you say, 'Behold, a
glutton and a drunkard, a friend of tax collectors and sinners!' "
(Luke 7:34). To part of this accusation Jesus pleads guilty. With
his whole life and death he declared himself to be the friend of
sinners.

These two glimpses of Jesus as friend reveal the paradox of his
peculiar love and righteousness. His passion for the holiness of
God created around him a fellowship of followers who were converted and called to righteousness, friends bound together in the
will of God through prayer, learning a new way that Jesus insisted
must "exceed the righteousness of the Pharisees" (Matt. 5:20). At
the same time the love of Jesus moved with an unpredictable freedom to expand the circle of friendship in the most unexpected directions. Those closest to him could never lay any exclusive claim
on his love. They also were compelled to open the circle (Matt.
19:13-14; Luke 9:12ff.; John 12:3-7). Jesus brought to bear a new
drive toward fellowship that shattered all the familiar human di-
visions, even the division between the religious and the "sinners."

To be a sign of Christ in the world, the Christian community
must live in the creative tension of this peculiar love. As a circle
of friends in Christ, sharing the intimacy of faith, there ought to
be a natural deepening and intensifying of relationships within the
community. In these reflections we have spoken for a close-knit

company of men and women whose lives are intricately bound to one another's. But in the open friendship of Jesus we are forbidden to try to guard our intimacy by closing the circle against "outsiders"—those who do not share our assumptions, our values, our familiar ways—or those whose suffering will interrupt our happy company.

The friendship of Jesus is not ours to manage. He says to his disciples, "You did not choose me, but I chose you and appointed you that you should go and bear fruit" (John 15:16). Our being together in Christ is grounded in nothing less than the overflowing love of God which pushes relentlessly and joyfully toward fellowship with creation. The outreach of Jesus and the consequent outreach of the friends of Jesus draws energy from this will-to-love of the eternal God.

Where does such love send us? How is the circle to be widened? Who are the "outsiders" we seek for the sake of the friendship of Jesus? Where does the *evangelizing community* begin?

EMBRACING THE SUFFERER

We once asked Eberhard Bethge, the friend and biographer of Dietrich Bonhoeffer, what he believed Bonhoeffer would be saying to the church today. Bethge concluded his response by saying: "At the end Bonhoeffer saw in his experience . . . that the church, with its dominating stature in the Western world, must now step down below."[1] That is, the church must once again learn to be the servant community.

This is the beginning point for the church's outreach. It does not move outward first of all to change the world or to win the world. "For the Son of man came not to be served but to serve" (Matt. 20:28). Only if the Christian community first of all seeks out those who are in greatest need does it make this intention clear: that it desires to embrace others simply in the will-toward-fellow-

---

[1]"Conversations with a Martyr's Friend: An Interview with Eberhard Bethge," *Mission Journal* 11 (September 1977): 69. For part one of the interview see *Mission Journal* 11 (August 1977): 27-30.

ship it has received from Jesus, not to clutch others for its own self-aggrandizement.

This simple offer of an uncomplicated love is desperately needed at a time when many churches have opted for a marketing of religion and a myriad of programs and "services" designed to attract the attractive. The church that quietly loves the "loveless" and the problem-laden says to the world: "We do not want to use you or deceive you. Do not give up altogether on the honesty of God's love." Only in this way can the church cease to be just another organization with a hidden strategy behind a smiling public face and instead become the friend whose heart is open and transparent in the world.

Many of us have participated in building "class" churches for the "haves," the "happy," and the fortunate. One can argue about how the situation has come about and how to dish out the blame, but the fact is that the whole pattern of common life in our churches too often excludes those who are isolated by their sufferings. For the community that claims allegiance to the suffering servant Christ, the sufferer has become the "outsider"! This betrayal of the gospel is the great burden of the churches.

We cannot do penance simply by new policy statements at a denominational level or by a sudden interest in the cause of justice in faraway places. Can we, in our own local communities of faith, break with this pattern of exclusion? Can we find a common life that brings us into a new association with those who are poor, in prison, emotionally ill, old and alone, sick or dying? Can we make any lively contact with those in whom Jesus especially dwells (Matt. 25:40)?

This is not really a question of the "betters" stooping to lift up the unfortunate. In a profound sense, it is the privileged who have much to gain from those whose lives are hard. Fellowship with the sufferer can only deepen our experience and save us from the narrow view and the boredom that attends the privileged life. Friendship with those who are poor can teach us the pretentiousness of our wealth-seeking and spur us on to a new simplicity that is a prerequisite for a new joy in the gospel. We were told that Antony Bloom, the leader of the Orthodox Church in England, was once asked by a young, well-to-do television interviewer, "What

really do I need that Christianity can offer?" His penetrating answer might serve as a profound prescription for the churches in
our society: "What you lack is the dimension of suffering."

But what can we do? What is it that we have to offer? In our
reflections we have tried to keep in mind the local, often small,
congregation without great resources. What can such a community do in the face of suffering? This is, of course, partly a straightforward and practical question that each community must answer
according to its gifts and its situation. But the question takes us
deeper than that.

After all, the mystery of suffering lies at the very heart of
Christian experience and faith. In the cross of Jesus Christ the moment of suffering, which had for all the ages been regarded as the
curse and cause of bitterness, came to be proclaimed as the supreme moment in the revelation of the love of God! As the price
he paid for his friendship with the "outsiders," the death of Jesus
came to be seen as the ultimate expression of friendship. "Greater
love has no man than this, that a man lay down his life for his
friends" (John 15:13). In the cross of Jesus, God the sufferer came
to weep with those who weep. In that shared sorrow a new dimension of joy is born. For if it is God who weeps with us, then
our pain, real and immovable as it is, cannot have the last word.
It cannot separate us; it is, mysteriously, a form of friendship with
the living God.

The Christian community will not be able to claim to eradicate much suffering. Certainly it ought not to attempt to explain
the mystery of seemingly purposeless pain. What it can do is to
receive the sufferer with reverence, in the spirit of the cross—to
hold to men and women in their time of suffering in the hope that
the moment of pain may bear fruit in the renewal and intensifi-
cation of human solidarity and trust in God. What the Christian
offers is simply a faith expressed in a tenacious presence, a presence that is in itself an invocation for the presence of God. When
God commands us to weep with those who weep (Rom. 12:15), we
are left in the poverty of faith, humbled by the mystery of suffering and by our incapacity to dictate life's terms. Such incapacity
is the truth under which human beings live. The cross dares us to

believe that even those moments of excruciating vulnerability can be received redemptively.

There are two ways to be found in the fellowship of Christ's sufferings. One way is to become one of life's victims, broken and helpless and alone. No one chooses that plight or is called to choose that way. We are taught to pray, "deliver us from evil." However, for such victims, Christ is near them in their sufferings; he has chosen them as his companions. And he has promised that God will judge the world on their behalf. The second way is open for us to choose. It is to be found standing alongside another who is suffering, caring in simple, direct ways as best we can, sharing the tears in the poverty of faith.

There is a natural pride in our society that glories in the fact that we have eradicated much disease, pain, and poverty. But such pride too quickly turns to blindness, so that those who continue to suffer among us become "invisible." And the loneliness becomes one with the texture of their pain. It is as if their suffering is an embarrassment, a flaw in our system, a technical problem to be eliminated by precise procedure or relegated to distant, ill-attended wards. In this cruelly paradoxical situation, the identity of a Christian and genuinely human community will be found in its capacity to receive the mystery of suffering as yet another moment in which the love of God is to be discovered.

EVANGELISM:
EXPANDING THE CIRCLE OF FRIENDSHIP

Only as we clarify the meaning of this open and uncomplicated love in the friendship of Jesus can we say anything meaningful about evangelism. How can the church's proclamation reach out unless its love reaches out? How can it call to the "outsiders" in the name of Christ if its life cannot embrace them in the love of Christ? God's Word is not a message shouted from a safe distance; it is the active and suffering human presence of Christ. Evangelism disconnected from this embracing love is not evangelism at all; it is mere religious propaganda, the sound of a clanging cymbal.

This is why in Jesus' initial proclamation of the kingdom of God there is no separation between the healing and helping love of God and the preaching of the gospel. When John the Baptist was languishing in prison he sent word to Jesus asking, "Are you he who is to come, or shall we look for another?" The reply of Jesus invoked the acts that every Jew could recognize as the prophetic signs of the coming kingdom of God. "Go and tell John what you have seen and heard: the blind receive their sight, the lame walk, lepers are cleansed, and the deaf hear, the dead are raised up, *the poor have the gospel* preached to them" (Luke 7:20-22, our emphasis). The love of Jesus for the sufferers and his announcement of the good news of God's love were like the fusion of music and words in the same gospel song. The poor in body and the poor in soul are embraced in the same new initiative of God's outpouring love.

It is in this exact context that Jesus cites the accusation that he was the "friend of sinners" (Luke 7:34). As we have seen, Jesus' table fellowship with the irreligious was a declaration that the friendship of God oversteps all barriers and suffers to bring all men and women around the single table of God's love. We have said this is the central image around which the Christian community finds its identity. Now we are saying it is also the picture of the church's life as an evangelizing community. It is not the sight of Peter preaching to the Jews on Pentecost or Paul preaching to the Greeks at Athens that forms the definitive picture of Christian evangelism. It is rather Jesus who lives and speaks in the incarnate love of God.

FROM FELLOWSHIP TO FAITH

The drive and goal of evangelism is a new fellowship—fellowship with God lived out in the new communion with God's people. There is an ultimate sense in which faith must precede fellowship, and repentance must open the way to the transformation that makes such communion real. So Jesus preaches: "the Kingdom of God is at hand; repent, and believe in the gospel" (Mark 1:15).

From this realization of the utter necessity of repentance and faith in receiving God's kingdom, the church naturally sees its responsibility to the unbelieving world as a call to the acceptance of its message. The model is utterly simple: the church propagates the gospel, and those who accept that message are incorporated into the fellowship of the church. The attitude of the Christian community to the unbeliever is then one of "attract and recruit," "convince and convert."

There are a number of reasons why such an understanding cannot do justice to the actual complexity of the task of evangelism. For one thing, it places Christians in a position of looking upon unbelievers in a less than fully human light. The unbeliever is no longer perceived in his or her wholeness. He or she becomes simply a "prospective Christian" or a religious "client." On the other hand, if the Christian cannot bear up under this "hidden agenda" in his or her relation with others, or if the challenge of evangelism is simply dismissed, then it is easy enough to corridor off one's faith and live in two separate sets of relationships. This is the way many Christians live. A second objection is that an "attract, inform, and convert" model can touch only a very narrow stratum of people, usually those who already have a religious "bent" and who share the same basic assumptions about life.

But the most serious objection to this way of conceiving evangelism is that it misconstrues the very character of Christian faith. Christianity is seen as if it were a truth or set of truths that can be pronounced upon from a distance, learned, and then lived. It is of course true that Christianity entails some claims which ought at some point to be confronted from a critical distance. But these claims are tied in their meaning to a whole life-process involving imagination, will, habits, and relationships. The Christian way is a new story, a new music, a new language. Therefore, *understanding assumes participation*. Coming to faith may entail having new dimensions of experience opened up, having one's vision transformed by new interpretations of life.

This understanding of faith is made clear enough in the Gospels. In the relation of Jesus of Nazareth to the chosen twelve, faith arises *along the way* in their fellowship with Jesus. Of course, there must have been something from their first moment of contact with him, some sense of the importance of his mission, that explains their willingness to follow him at all. But their attachment to him was marked by all sorts of misunderstandings. It is an obvious but significant point that Peter's confession, "You are the Christ," comes not at the beginning of the story but in the middle. Even then the disciples do not comprehend the significance of their confession. Long before the disciples called Jesus "Christ" they called him simply "master" or "teacher." Faith grew out of fellowship and confrontation with the unique humanity of Jesus in the shared life of his company.

What of Jesus' encounter with the "sinners"? Each meeting entailed a call to repentance. But repentance was not a hurdle to be leapt over in order to find access to Jesus. Repentance rather erupted as a new possibility in life, because Jesus was present bringing a new unexpected forgiveness. The call to repentance is grounded in the act of fellowship. We can begin to understand this if we can imagine Zacchaeus, the woman at the well, and the prostitute with her alabaster box eventually coming to stand within the Christian community singing, "Jesus is Lord!" And it all began in their initial discovery that Jesus is friend.

In the Gospels the first "step to salvation" is the friendship of Jesus, the compelling claim of his company. It is a step Jesus himself takes. Then in the company of Jesus the transformation of life emerges as a new possibility, and the mystery of his identity comes to light. From fellowship to faith, from friendship to repentance— that is the sequence of the gospel. It is his presence that makes good the gospel claim, "the kingdom of God draws near," and that then makes viable the call, "repent and believe the gospel" (Mark 1:15).

Christian theology has in fact always held to the truth that Christ's presence always goes before faith and that faith rests upon that presence. This is the doctrine of "prevenient grace" taught by Paul, developed by Augustine, and held dear by the reformers.[2] Wherever one comes to confess Christ, the Holy Spirit of God in

---

[2]The belief in a "prevenient" presence of God that precedes faith underlies Augustine's account of his own conversion in the *Confessions*. See also John Calvin's *Institutes of the Christian Religion* 3.2.

Christ has in fact been present all along, nourishing that faith into existence. "No one can say 'Jesus is Lord' except by the Holy Spirit" (1 Cor. 12:3).

This doctrine is easily understood in too abstract and individualistic a way if such "presence" is conceived in terms *only* of some "interior" witness in the individual heart. After all, there is in history a presence, a visible communion in the fellowship of Christ, that is also a "communion in the Holy Spirit" (2 Cor. 13:14). Wherever men and women are gathered in Christ's sacrificial love, there the grace of God is "prevenient" and the possibility of faith is held out.

THE EVANGELIZING COMMUNITY

All of this leads us to the awareness that stands behind all we desire to say about evangelism. That is, it is the life of the Christian community that is the means and method of evangelism. This life, nourished and shared in the presence of Christ, holds open that dimension of grace in which men and women may discover the identity of Christ and call him their Lord. For many outsiders, coming to faith will depend on whether or not they can be claimed by the reality of love in the Christian fellowship. Faith arises in fellowship, in human solidarity in the way and will of Christ. Evangelism is not some additional activity appended to our individual Christian lives and actions; it is an impulse that arises out of Christian community at the most basic level. It is the broadening of the circle of friendship in Christ. It means welcoming the outsider in the open friendship of Jesus.

There is, of course, nothing new in what we are saying. For all of us who "grew up" into Christian faith, it was the life of the Christian community that bore us along. Long before we were ready to "own" and assent to faith, we were held, however feebly, in that exchange of love and grace that bound us to Jesus. For us, quite simply, fellowship preceded faith.

Preachers are fond of saying that the most eloquent sermon is the Christian life lived well in the world. No doubt there is power in a single life lived gracefully and lovingly. But the New Testament is slow to speak at all about the individual Christian life. The sign of Christ in the world, the body of Christ, is not this or that life, no matter how exemplary; it is our common life in the *koinonia* of God. Its power to bear Christ's presence arises not from some exemplary moral superiority, even less from its power to influence the minds of others. It is quite simply the mystery of *koinonia*—that exchange of love in the concrete struggles of life that rehearses again and again the sacrificial love of the cross. If the stranger to Christ is held in that exchange, words like "salvation," "forgiveness," "sin," and "reconciliation" begin to take on flesh. Faith becomes a possibility.

Jesus Christ was a friend to the outsider and welcomed "sinners" in the name of God. Can the Christian community welcome the outsider? Is ours a love that strives to jump all the human barriers, even the barriers between belief and unbelief? These are the questions that the task of evangelism puts to us.

But will those who do not share the Christian faith desire to "come to church"? Some will, if "coming to church" means being drawn into a genuinely human company in open friendship; if it means discovering a place to celebrate the goodness of life in real festivity; if it means learning to share their own suffering and, what may be more important, being challenged to help to bear the sufferings of others. As they come, they will be, like those in the Gospels, in all sorts of different attitudes in their relation to Jesus Christ. Some will find in him a challenge to their strength and courage, a call to live more humanly in the world, long before they learn their need for his forgiveness. They will call him "teacher" long before they call him "Lord." Others will limp along in his love and forgiveness before they learn to obey him. Some will come blinded by their pain and confusion to anything other than their need for human affection. As they come—sharing in our meals, joining in our discussions, working by our side, listening to the reading of Scripture, wondering at our confession of faith around the Lord's table, joining in the mutual exchange of hospitality— some, not all, but some, will be grasped by that Spirit which alone enables one to say, "Jesus is Lord."

For some Christians this will all sound like a frustratingly inconclusive, formless, and unpredictable way of going about evangelism. So it is. But the real heart of the challenge is not finding an occasion to set forth Christian teaching. Through books, broadcasts, billboards, magazines, and T.V. interviews, the words are endlessly repeated. It is the living context of faith that is lacking. Evangelism begins with a deep respect for the mystery of faith and for the freedom of Christ to call his own however he chooses.

> In the final sense, salvation is not through works or through faith but *through Christ*—that is, through Him and through the whole world of love, service and self-sacrifice which he embodies, pioneers and empowers.[3]

Now we are back once again at the beginning, to the question that underlies all that we have said in this book. What sort of community is the Christian congregation to be? How can we be a genuinely human family that is a sign of that "whole world of love, service and self-sacrifice which Christ embodies, pioneers and empowers?" It also becomes clear that everything we have said in our reflections is a word about evangelism. In this task there is simply no separating doing from being. To live in the friendship of Jesus is to dwell in a home with the doors and windows open to the world of men and women in their suffering and in their need of God.

To speak as we have about evangelism also calls into question our willingness to be challenged and changed in our churches by the presence of the outsiders. This is the difference between evangelism and mere propaganda. Propagandists speak from a distance and are not touched or moved by those they address. But the evangelizing community speaks to women and men face to face; it desires to be near them in the passion (the capacity to be moved) of Jesus. The humbling thing is that in friendship with the irreligious, Christians will often find a love, a self-giving, an honest truth-seeking, even an intuitive grasp of the meaning of Christ that is sorely lacking within the community—just as when Jesus was once confronted by a pagan and compelled to say, "Not even in Israel have I found such faith" (Matt. 8:5-13).

---

[3]John Vincent, *Christ and Methodism* (London: Epworth Press, 1965) 32.

BEING SILENT FOR CHRIST

Nothing we have said has been intended to dull the urgency of the task of proclaiming the love of Christ. The Christian community has a message to proclaim, a story to tell, a truth to make clear. We are not speaking for a fuzzy, simplistic tolerance that is a mask for sheer confusion and indifference. To open our life to others demands rather that we know where we stand. It means a deeper security and faith that can be found only in deeper worship and frequent prayer. It demands a strengthening of community. There is an inherent militancy in Christian faith that happily assumes the partisan spirit and says with Paul, "we believe and so we speak" (2 Cor. 4:13). But Christians are under a special imperative to stick close to the "flesh," to speak incarnationally, to tie word and deed together as a single sign of Christ.

According to the Gospels, the very first ones to publicly acknowledge Christ were the demons, who knew him by his power over them. But Jesus' command to them is unequivocal: "Be silent!" (Mark 1:25; 3:11-12). Later, when Peter confesses by inspiration, "You are the Christ," he and the other disciples are also silenced. "And [Jesus] charged them to tell no one about him" (Mark 8:29, 30). The reason is made clear in the words of Jesus that immediately follow the injunction to silence.

> And he began to teach them that the Son of man must suffer many things, and be rejected by the elders and the chief priests and the scribes, and be killed, and after three days rise again. And he said this plainly. And Peter took him, and began to rebuke him. But turning and seeing his disciples, he rebuked Peter, and said, "Get behind me, Satan! For you are not on the side of God, but of men." And he called to him the multitude with his disciples, and said to them, "If any man would come after me, let him deny himself and take up his cross and follow me (Mark 8:31-34).

Christ must suffer in the world before the meaning of his messianic identity can be unveiled. Likewise, the community of disciples must make common cause with the suffering Son of man before it can bear witness to that identity. Any merely verbal witness is premature. It cannot serve the purposes of Christ in his suffering; therefore, it merely belittles the gospel and so becomes to that extent "demonic."

The suffering servant Christ did not come into the world with a great shout. He came silently, God's whisper upon earth. "He had no form or comeliness that we should look at him, and no beauty that we should desire him. . . . He was oppressed, and he was afflicted, yet he opened not his mouth" (Isa. 53:2,7). Even in his resurrection glory Christ shunned the dazzling display. He made his quiet approach as a friend. In his presence along the road, at table, at the seaside, he opened the eyes of men and women to see and believe.

The church that is the servant of this presence is not called to fill the world with the sound of religious verbiage or to assault the world with religious fervor. It is called first to serve and to suffer with. In the serving and the suffering, many will find a place of welcome and friendship. Then the moment will be granted to speak the gracious word, "seasoned with salt, so that you may know how you ought to answer every one" (Col. 4:6). And some will hear and believe the gospel.

9

A COMMUNITY
IN WORSHIP

*Give diligence therefore to come together more fre-
quently for thanksgiving and glory to God, for when
you are frequently together in one place, the powers
of Satan are destroyed and his destructiveness is nul-
lified by the concord of your faith.*

Ignatius

We have written from the beginning of these pages out of
hope for the rediscovery of the Christian congregation. This does
not mean the rediscovery of a system, a polity, an institution, a
bureaucracy, a dogma, a technique. Nor can it mean business as
usual at Main Street Church, which seeks our attendance and our
money but which changes nothing, confronts nothing, dreams
nothing, suffers nothing, and serves nothing. Our task is nothing
less than the rediscovery of the fullness of our humanity in the redemptive presence of Jesus Christ, a new way of being in the world
for the congregation. We have seen that this means: community
over individualism, authenticity over pretense, sacramental living over compartmentalized existence; the rediscovery of the
wholeness of persons instead of soul/body dualism; the whole-

ness of the church rather than a clergy/laity bifurcation; the rediscovery of the fullness of the incarnation of truth over the emptiness of words alone; the rediscovery of wisdom over thoughtlessness, being over function, involvement over isolationism, and service over self-interest.

We end where we began—with the promise of the presence of Jesus where two or three are gathered in his name. The celebration of this sacramental reality arises in the gathered community at worship—at the Lord's Table and in the Lord's Word—and extends that worship into every aspect of life in the Lord's world. If the Christian congregation is to be a zone of freedom then it exists to keep the world open for the relationship between God and creation and to be a place where human life can be liberated from bondage to the principalities and powers. If the context of our world is one of idolatrous seduction then the worship of the one true God becomes more, not less, important. In order to rediscover the Christian celebration of life, in order to drink from the refreshing waters of the wellsprings of faith, in order to sing the song of our confession in word and deed that "Jesus is Lord," it is imperative for the congregation to understand that Christian life and worship—*community* and *communion*—are the inseparable tandem in the yoke of salvation and freedom.

Worship is the way of being in the world for the community of faith, marking the center and circumference of our life and ministry together. *Worship is all the Christian congregation does.* It is crucial that our understanding of worship be expansive enough to cut through the false dichotomies we have allowed to creep into and overrun our Christian experience. It is just because of such false dichotomies that we can be "faithful church members" while at the same time serving the values of the old order in ethics, politics, and life style.

In the New Testament there is a cluster of seven or eight words for the concept of worship; they range in meaning from reverence, awe, and devotion, to service, life style, giving, and social action. To conceive of worship as a total way of life is not so strange. One worships, at least in part, to answer the question "Who do I choose to be?" Likewise, who one chooses to be reveals the object of one's worship. *Everyone* worships—the question is only who or what do we worship?

When the powers of the world demand unconditional allegiance and assume people should assign them ultimate value, then the worship of God becomes a radical act. The greatest single threat to the principalities and powers comes in the worship of God and in the spoken and lived prayer of the community, "Your kingdom come." This understanding of worship means that we must break through what Daniel Migliore has called the "deadening alternatives" with which all of us are familiar: "prayer or politics; transformation of individuals or transformation of social conditions; a personal or a political interpretation of the gospel."[1]

The congregation cannot abandon what has always been essential to Christian spirituality; nor can it abandon, through a world-denying piety, the pains and aspirations of its society. For example, *prayer* will bind the community not only to God but to the world through creative intercession. *Meditative recollection* will probe the meaning of the cross of Christ that is planted in the earth. There the Son of man died for the sons and daughters of all humanity. As a social outcast, his death was easily justified by the political and religious system of his day. Surely, if we are in this Christ, then such meditation can only deepen our sensitivity to the victims of injustice and death, and deepen our suspicion of the exercise of power in any temporal realm. *Bible reading* will become not simply a learning of the ancient stories but the listening for a living word which breaks into our present story in judgment and grace. Nor can we *eat the bread and drink the wine* in the open feast of him who ate with sinners, the poor, and the outcasts, while at the same time remaining an exclusive religious and socially acceptable community. The *exercise of the gifts of the spirit* will surely lead to critical analysis, discernment, prophetic insight, and action in the midst of the religious, social, economic, and political forces of our time.

---

[1]Daniel L. Migliore, *Called to Freedom* (Philadelphia: Westminster Press, 1980) 83.

We have stressed the breadth of meaning in "worship," and we have spoken for a world-engaging rather than a world-denying piety. The point can hardly be overstated. There remains, after all, plenty of scope in the contemporary church for applying the prophetic accusation, "they honor me with their lips, while their hearts are far from me" (Isa. 29:13). We well remember being in an inner-city church on Palm Sunday when the morning liturgy called for the congregation to process around the sanctuary carrying palms. After the service, the pastor was extolling the way the congregation had joined in. "Yes," he said, without apparent irony, "that was the church in action!" One got the impression that for this pastor worship was not a way of life but a substitute for living.

But there is another side to this question. Even the strongest insistence that worship involves the whole of our living cannot obscure the uniqueness of the *constituting act* of the congregation: the gathering together for the specific space-and-time-filling act of the liturgy of Word and sacrament. Worship, in this most specific sense, is the native soil of Christian existence. Christian identity, cohesive community, and spiritual sensitivity will wither and die without it.

This must be urged in a book like this one, because those who argue as we have that our congregations ought to be intentional, acting, protesting, and witnessing communities too often seem to relegate the common worship to a utilitarian role in support of relevant discipleship. The worship assembly is regarded as hardly more than a rallying point from which we all are urged to hurry into the "real" world to do the "real" work of being Christians. But this functional understanding of the Christian assembly misconstrues the meaning of both worship and discipleship.

Worship as substitute for life or worship as a functional sideshow: these have too often been the "deadening alternatives" in our approach to the worship assembly, and the true liturgy of the people of God has suffered. One of the encouraging developments in the contemporary church is that we are breaking out of this bind. Many factors are making such a change possible. Not least among them is the new mutuality that has grown up among Protestant, Roman Catholic, and Orthodox Christians. There is also a deep questioning concerning the very nature of the church resulting from the breakdown of the familiar church-and-culture alliances. New historical knowledge has furthered our understanding of ancient Christian worship, sweeping away some of the old assumptions. Finally, the abiding spiritual thirst of men and women has once again thrown off the secular disguise. For many Protestants, all these developments have taken stimulating form in the recent documents of the Faith and Order Commission of the World Council of Churches.[2]

What then is transpiring when the Christian congregation gathers for worship? How may we find again the ancient confidence that when Christians "are frequently together in one place, the powers of Satan are destroyed . . . by the concord of your faith"? How can we acknowledge and claim Christ's power and presence in our gathering? And how does the service of Word and sacrament stamp its claim across the whole life of the dispersed people of God?

THE CONGREGATION AS SIGN

If we are to understand that *worship is all the Christian community does*, we must grasp the truth that the congregation has no meaning other than its call to be a sign of Christ in the world. As Wolfhart Pannenberg has recently said, the church exists to symbolize; and "to restore the feeling for the thoroughly symbolic nature of the church means to recover its spiritual reality."[3] It is not simply that the church employs the sacraments. Rather, the community in its being and doing is itself a sacrament, a sign, a living transparency through which the very words and deeds of Jesus

---

[2]See especially *Baptism, Eucharist, and Ministry: Faith and Order Paper No. 111* (Geneva: World Council of Churches, 1982); and *Ecumenical Perspectives on Baptism, Eucharist, and Ministry: Faith and Order Paper No. 116*, ed. Max Thurian (Geneva: World Council of Churches, 1983).

[3]Wolfhart Pannenberg, *Christian Spirituality* (Philadelphia: Westminster Press, 1983) 38.

shine. This sacramental character is as true of the simplest act of Christian obedience as it is of corporate worship.

The life of the congregation cannot be evaluated simply by its utility to this or that agenda or by its accomplishments. Especially the small congregation struggling in the center of a vast urban expanse must cling to this truth if it is not to falter at its own relative powerlessness. At the same time, we need to remember that to call something a symbol or sign is not to demean it. Symbols can be as practical and effective as weapons or tools.

The sign of the congregation can be effectual because it partakes of the same Spirit that animated the words and deeds of Jesus, which were themselves signs in the world of the coming kingdom of God (Luke 11:20). Each word spoken and each deed done in the name of Jesus Christ repeats the litany, "Your kingdom come." The sacramental nature of the congregation means, therefore, that our community life is filled with the eschatological tension that marked the deeds of Jesus. We live for a new order that has not fully dawned but is sure to come.

Only if we fail to grasp this "signing" character of the church's life can we call into question the integrity and efficacy of its liturgy. But if we recognize the community's sacramental identity, we will no longer say feebly that worship simply strengthens us to live better for Christ. We must see that the liturgy—the gathering around the Bible, bread, and wine—is the very pattern of our existence in the world. Gathered in worship the community is simply itself, with no excuse for being except the grace and promise of God, no message to utter except the word Christ gives, no deed to perform except the self-offering Christ makes present to us in his sacred meal, no hope to offer except the promise of his presence and his coming.

THE SANCTIFICATION OF THE HUMAN

Christian worship is the human worship of God in Christ, the new human being. Christians, therefore, are not intended to leave their simple human needs and longings behind when they gather. Worship is rather an offering up of our humanity to the God who created us. With our eyes open to the human character of our liturgy, perhaps we can be made more sensitive to the power of our worship to embrace, dignify, and transform our daily existence.

The sanctification of our togetherness. There are all kinds of togetherness. People come together to achieve a common task and to learn from one another. Sometimes they come together because they are afraid and they seek the comfort of a crowd. They come together simply to enjoy each other's company. Our many ways of togetherness have their impetus in some human need, desire, or demand. Because that is true, our ways of being together are fragile and vulnerable, and they often have a kind of desperation about them. How much pain and confusion flows from the breakdown of our togetherness. How often our togetherness degenerates into a devouring or a suffocating of one another. How easily our togetherness wounds others by exclusion.

In Christ we are called to learn anew to be together and to be together in a new way. Christian togetherness does not derive its original driving force simply from our needs as we see them and seek to assuage them. It starts rather from the word of Christ, who comes among us, calls us around him, stands between one believer and another, and makes us one communion of women and men in the world. To put the matter in traditional terms, Christian togetherness has a transcendent quality about it. Without this transcendence, community—especially religious community—can be a suffocating experience full of nothing but demands to fulfill, jobs to do, and troubles to take care of. For many there is nothing more exhausting than that mere sociability that assumes we are all supposed to like one another and be together all the time. No wonder many who have set out to build effective, close-knit communities have "burnt out" before very long.

The gathering for worship is in itself an invocation of Christ to grace our togetherness by his presence. When we stand or sit or kneel together in worship, the Christ among us "takes responsibility" for our solidarity, intensifying our responsibility for one another even while he paradoxically frees us from our compulsive demands over one another by locating our togetherness in him rather than in ourselves. Because Christ is our solidarity, we believe that even through the obstacles of our failures and misun-

derstandings and inabilities, our togetherness is secured for
eternity.

Although the communion of the Holy Spirit that Christ estab-
lishes among us is a mystery and cannot be defined, there are ways
we can recognize the "lifting up" of our togetherness in the liturgy. For example, in worship our sense of the others is immediately expanded and saved from a suffocating parochialism,
because when we gather at Christ's table, we become aware that
this is the place where, all around the city and the world, Christ's
people are collected. If Christ is present with us, then so are all
those who down through the ages have been gathered in Christ—
who now in heaven and on earth surround him in fidelity and ad-
oration. For the small, struggling community, this sense of the
spacious communion of the saints can be a liberation from the
cramped "tyranny of the urgent" that can sometimes descend on
the community bent on doing God's will.

Alongside this experience of linkage with all the faithful, the
gathered community can experience an expanded togetherness
through its Christ-given solidarity with the world. The Christ who
is present in the community came because God so loved the world.
He came to live and die for sinners. He will come again to transform his creation in his resurrection power. So the congregation
of Christ does not worship huddled with its back toward the world.
The Christian community, in fact, represents that world as it
awaits the eschatological work of God. That is, the gathered church
anticipates and signifies the whole redeemed human community.
The community gathered in Christ lives an intercessory existence
as the voice of longing for true human solidarity.

This entails both affirmation and denial. In many places men
and women are now reacting to a destructive individualism and
are longing for togetherness and solidarity. The Christian community affirms this longing and shares in both the successes and
failures that mark our efforts to be a genuine human society. And
yet, the church exists to signify that all forms of human togetherness—all human society—is provisional, pointing like a prayer
toward God's eschatological gathering. We gather to pray, "Your
kingdom come." With that petition our gathering becomes a protest and sign that the kingdom of human togetherness cannot be

grasped by violence or ingenuity or social engineering, but must be awaited and received in faith.

The sanctification of time. In the regular and recurring gathering for worship, the human experience of life in time is taken up and transformed in Christ. The Christian shares with all other people the passage of time, and the passage of time leads to change and death. If we are to understand the frantic quality of much modern life, we must discern the fear and dread with which human beings, caught in the race against death, fear time. Thomas Merton has written of the anxiety of the "modern pagan," the "child of technology," who "lives not only below the level of grace, but below the level of nature—below his own humanity. . . . In such a world, a man's life is no longer even a seasonal cycle. It's a linear flight into nothingness, a flight from reality and from God, without purpose and without objective, except to keep moving, to keep from having to face reality."[4] If Merton's description fits no one's life exactly, it partially identifies many modern persons well enough. But to live a genuinely human life is to be able to live graciously in time.

When a person enters the Christian community, they ought to be taken up into a new rhythm of life in which time is no longer the enemy. For Christ has "tamed" time in his conquest of human death. In Christ, time is no longer simply a passing; it is filled with the spirit of pilgrimage. Time is no longer the thief that steals away our happiness; it is the herald announcing the approach of a destination.

Christian worship breathes with this sense of transformed time. Earlier we argued for lectionary preaching. We have also pointed out how keeping the special feast days in the Christian calendar can help to punctuate the community life with the spirit of festivity. Here the traditional Christian marking of time is once again found to be immanently relevant to the task of building a humanity-nourishing Christian life. In ordering time according to the

---

[4]Thomas Merton, *Meditations On Liturgy* (London and Oxford: Mowbrays, 1976) 31; originally published in U.S.A. as *Seasons of Celebration* (Magnolia MA: Peter Smith, 1965).

gospel of Christ, the church is instinctively taking hold of God's gift of time renewed in Jesus Christ. In Christ time itself is taken up by prayer and praise and is infused with a sacramental character. "Jesus has made this ebb and flow of light and darkness, activity and rest, birth and death, the sign of a higher life, a life which we live in him, a life which knows no decline, and a day which does not fall into darkness."[5]

Sacramental time-keeping has received more emphasis in some church traditions than in others. But across the whole spectrum of the church through the ages, Catholic and Protestant alike, the Christian community has held on to the sign of the Lord's Day. Contemporary Protestant ecclesiology has shown a new interest in the meaning and relevance of this sign for the church in our society. Based on passages like Romans 14:5 and Colossians 2:16, and in reaction to the almost pagan servitude to "holy days" that marked the life of the church in their time, the sixteenth-century reformers in some of their writings came very near to abandoning the sign of Sunday in the name of Christian freedom.[6] But no one in the ancient church seems to have construed Paul's words in opposition to an observance of this day as the festal day of Christian worship. The New Testament suggests that the Lord's Day (the phrase first appears in Rev. 1:10) became linked very early with the observance of the Lord's Supper (Acts 20:7). In 1 Corinthians 16:2 the offering for the poor in Jerusalem (whether at home or in a common collection) takes on a quasisacramental character through its being linked with the first day of the week.

The meaning of this day is of course tied to the resurrection of Jesus on the first day of the week, which inaugurated a new "first day" in the history of the new creation. This "first day" is that

---

[5]Ibid., 29.

[6]See Luther's Larger Catechism on the fourth commandment and The Augsburg Confession, VII. For Calvin's view see his *Institutes* 2.8.33, 34. Both Luther and Calvin were eager to separate the observance of Sunday from all hint of legalism and tended to regard it as a mere expedient. Karl Barth faults the reformers for taking a practical rather than a theological interpretation of the day. See *Church Dogmatics* 3, 1:4.

perpetual "today" in which the church is called to live (Heb. 3:13). The sign of the Easter existence is the gathering of the community each first day.

The meaning of the Easter time in which the church lives is deepened if we do not artificially sever the Lord's Day from its roots in the Sabbath. The anti-Jewish polemic in the early church fathers and, again, in the writings of the reformers forced a sharp division between the two days. But theology since has searched for a more balanced view.[7] The change of the festive day in the ancient Christian community from the Sabbath to the first day does, of course, mark the coming of a radically new experience. The new wine demanded a new wineskin. Yet, the celebration of this new day carried with it associations from the Sabbath. As the writer of the Epistle to the Hebrews makes clear, the "sabbath rest" is a theme dear to Christian as well as Jewish theology. Christians are urged to recognize that through faith in Jesus we enter the promised Sabbath of God.

An indication of the continuity between the two days is that the ancient gentile church so readily adopted the Hebrew sabbatical reckoning of time according to seven days. The New Testament phrase "first day of the week" is an idiomatic translation that means literally, "the first of the sabbaths," that is, the first in a series of days determined by the Sabbath. This is all the more remarkable, since no seven-day division of time was familiar in the Roman Empire of the time.[8] Thus the sign of Sunday became one of the distinctive marks of Christian identity.

Our purpose here is not to get entangled in the complicated issues involved in the relation of Sunday to the Sabbath. But we are struck by the immediate relevance of the theme of rest to the Christian church in our society. The point has not been missed by theologians as they have recovered a theology of the Lord's Day.

---

[7]A well-documented and useful survey of Protestant opinions as well as some stimulating theological construction has been provided by Paul K. Jewett, The Lord's Day (Grand Rapids MI: William B. Eerdmans, 1971).

[8]Ibid., 76.

Alfred De Querrain, who greatly influenced Karl Barth's discussion of the subject, has written,

> A church which waits for her Lord and anticipates the revelation of his lordship over all the kingdoms of this world, will never abandon the sign of Sunday with an appeal to Christian freedom. This day proclaims loudly to all the world, even the modern heathen world, that man through his own care and work can never build the kingdom of eternal glory.[9]

In a society that everywhere reduces human life with the demand to produce, that glorifies the successful and deifies wealth, the call to cease and simply to rest becomes an imperative of the gospel. The free keeping of the festive day in the sanctuary of worship and fellowship signifies the rest from ambition, greed, and the frenzied activity that diminishes our lives.

But there is more to it than that. For the rest Christ brings is also the abandoning of *all* self-justifying activity—including the attempts of the Christian community to establish its own relevance in the world. "Rest" in this sense, is hardly the mere ceasing from activity. It is a repose filled with the dynamic resuscitation of our slothful spirits by the Easter life of Jesus. Such dynamism begins not in the quest for accomplishment, not even in any of our carefully formed agendas for discipleship, but only in the resting of faith in Jesus.

The community gathers to pray, "Give us *this day*. . . ." In that prayer, all its time is taken up. The "first day" of Christ's Easter life permeates all its days. The body of Christ which is broken in the world on the six days is restored again in wholeness on the first day.

The sanctification of space. The gathering of the congregation for worship in one place is the sign of the empirical reality of Christ's body in the world. The "sacred place" may help to make room in the heart to discern Christ's presence in all the places we live. If we are not to overlook the power of this sign, we will have to pay attention to the simple human needs of people.

---

[9]Translated and quoted ibid., 97.

We recall the middle-aged widow whose life as a fulltime social worker and mother of three was far from easy. Her household was often in disorder and her life cluttered with a mound of responsibilities. She came early one Sunday to sit in our simple chapel, and soon the tears began to fall. When someone asked her what was wrong she replied haltingly that simply the quiet and order of the place, in such stark contrast to what she felt was the chaos of her life, had made her both sad and joyful in the same moment and allowed her emotions to flow.

"Let there always be quiet, dark churches," writes Thomas Merton, drawing on his catholic sensitivity, "in which men can take refuge. . . . There, even when they do not know how to pray, at least they can be still and breathe easily. . . ."[10] His words are not without relevance for even the small congregation with few material resources.

Whenever Christians get serious about practical discipleship, there are some who may fall into that grim piety that would almost ban beauty, order, and quietude as a superfluous distraction from the real business of Christian living. They seem to resent the fact that the community of Christ, like every other human family, might find joy in a "house" filled with light and warmth, associations and memories, the spirit of commonality and the symbols of the faith. Some rational soul is always quick to point out that God, the omnipresent One, ought not to be fixedly associated with this or that place. But there is also a simple wisdom in Friedrich von Hügel's reminder that "It is man who worships, not God; but man here below at least, experiences in space as he does in time; one space is not the same to him as another place. . . . Cease to worship God in particular places, and your worship will become less vivid, less concentrated."[11]

---

[10]Thomas Merton, *New Seeds of Contemplation* (London: Burns and Oates, 1962) 64.

[11]Friedrich von Hügel, *Essays and Addresses on the Philosophy of Religion: Second Series* (London and Toronto: J. M. Dent & Sons, 1928) 67.

It is constantly said (but not often enough listened to) that the churches have spent far too much money on church buildings and that these properties are the signs of worldly status rather than signs of Christ among us. It is true; the community's gift of "sanctified space" needs urgently to be disciplined by and harmonized with the crucial demands on resources. But it has to be remembered that in this matter most of us cannot start at the beginning, even if we wanted to. The question for us is how not to squander the gift of place bequeathed to us, how to offer it to God.

A creative balance with regard to sanctified space will always be summed up for us in the story told about Taizé, the contemporary ecumenical monastic community in France. In the early days of their community life the brothers built with their own hands a simple but beautiful church for their common worship. But as the crowds of visitors to Taizé swelled, the little church was often overcrowded. One particular day, as young people from all over Europe journeyed to Taizé for several days of prayer, the brothers decided—as a sign of welcome and as an expression of the provisional nature of all such places—to then and there knock out one wall of the church! The Christian community may be called upon from time to time to knock down (literally or figuratively) the walls of its churches. But such gestures will have little meaning unless we have first learned to value and employ this gift and sign.

The sanctification of the body. The fourth-century church historian Eusebius tells us that Saint James had knees like a camel because he knelt so long in prayer.[12] And Athanasius once remarked that we were created with hands to pray with.[13] This ancient assumption that prayer is as much a bodily as an intellectual act sounds strange to people grown used to theoretically regarding their bodies as mere "husks" of the true "inner" selves. We say "theoretically" because most of us indeed treat our bodies with great practical care even if our language remains dualistic. Thankfully, even in the theoretical realm, contemporary thought is

---

[12]Eusebius, *Ecclesiastical History* 2.23.78.

[13]Athanasius, *Contra Gentes* 4.

throwing off the mind/body dualism that has dominated our philosophy and psychology now for at least three hundred years. We are now in a better position to begin to recapture the Hebrew sense of human wholeness that marks biblical piety and worship.[14]

From a modern perspective, it is remarkable how much significance the New Testament gives to the human body. Especially Paul, who had to combat a first-century form of dualism not so different from that which has marked modern thought, consistently focuses on the organic reality of human existence. The body of the Christian, Paul insists, is the very temple of the Holy Spirit. Our bodies are "members of Christ," therefore we are told to "glorify God in your body" (1 Cor. 6:19-20). The apostle considered that the scars of persecution on his own flesh were the very "marks of Jesus" (Gal. 6:17) and were a mysterious participation in the ongoing sufferings of Christ himself for the sake of the church (Col. 1:24). The content of the Christian hope of salvation can be summed up by Paul as the "redemption of our bodies" (Rom. 8:23). Surely, for him, the resurrection of the body, no matter what sort of theoretical difficulty it raises, was a nonnegotiable tenet of the faith (1 Cor. 15:35-58). For human beings in Christ are not destined to be angels or "spirits" but are redeemed in their created, mysterious, psychosomatic wholeness. Therefore when Paul writes, "present your bodies as a living sacrifice" (Rom. 12:1), he envisions a life offered to God in all its historical, social, and organic dimensions. In other words, he envisions a fully human response to the mercies of God incarnate in Christ. The New English Bible's rendering, "present yourselves," is an attempt to capture the breadth of Paul's meaning, but "selves" is liable to be read far too "spiritually" by the reader today. This injunction to present our bodies to God follows the believer into every nook of life. But does it not have a simple human relevance for the specific acts of prayer and worship?

---

[14]An excellent discussion of the wide-ranging effects of a false dualism in theology and piety is provided in the much neglected work of L. S. Thornton, *Revelation and the Modern World* (London: Dacre Press, 1950) 29-91, 106-110.

Some of us, whose Christian life was first nurtured by a highly rationalistic and "inner" piety, have had to learn through the pains of experience what we might call the "priority of bodily presence" in prayer and worship. We have had to learn with C. S. Lewis not to try to be more spiritual than God! As with the athlete whose skill resides as much in the limbs as in the mind, like the child who can hardly learn the meaning of love without physical tenderness, like the author who often does not know what she wants to say until her hand has grasped the pen and is moving freely across the page, so sometimes the spirit and the will are frozen until we are able simply to make ourselves bodily present in prayer.

The church instinctively bears witness to this fully human embrace of piety and worship by the sacraments of baptism and the Lord's Supper. These acts are the "body language" of the church. Like the touch, the kiss, the embrace, they bear witness to that hidden juncture where flesh and spirit meet in the power of the Creator Spirit to make life. In these acts our bodies, and even the inanimate creation (water, bread, wine), are caught up in the strange ways of grace.

The physical gathering of the congregation is itself a bodily gesture indicating that we have heard the call to serve Christ's presence and to be his body in the world. In worship we literally dump our lives and our corporate life before God, making our community bodily present to God and to one another, invoking Christ to gather us up and make of us his body.

Giving attention to human wholeness in worship helps us understand how natural it is for the church to employ the whole range of human gifts and responses in worship: music, gesture, symbol, light, and all that delights us and naturally evokes our thought and emotion. The Word around which the congregation gathers registers its power over us through the words of Scripture, through the exhortations of the preacher, through the theological impact of image and idea on the imagination and intellect. But the Word, who after all once took up bodily presence in this world, can also breathe and speak in the "logic" of the senses. For the Word once took bread and ceremonially broke it before his congregation, called it his body, and said, *do this*. . . .

Earlier in this chapter we spoke of worship as the dynamic resting of the congregation in Christ. Now a similar image arises— the child absorbed in the energy and delight of play. We are not suggesting here the all-too-frequent and irresponsible attempts to manufacture emotions and responses in the awkward, studied informality of some worship "experiments." The games of children are, in fact, sometimes highly ceremonial! We are thinking rather about the deep, participatory, festive joy that can emerge if we forget ourselves in the worship of God.

It is true that Christian living ought to be marked by what J. Christiaan Beker has recently called the "passion of sobriety," which is ever purposeful in discerning the duty of practical love.[15] But is there not also room for the community to "joyfully taste of the sober drunkenness of the Spirit"?[16] It is the purpose of worship to teach us not to "see purposes everywhere,"

> not to be desirous of being over-clever and grown-up, but to understand simplicity in life. The soul must learn to abandon, at least in prayer, the restlessness of purposeful activity; it must learn to waste time for the sake of God, and to be prepared for the sacred game with sayings and thoughts and gestures, without always immediately asking "why?" and "wherefore?" It must learn not to be continually yearning to do something, to attack something, to accomplish something useful, but to play the divinely ordained game of the liturgy in liberty and beauty and holy joy before God.[17]

A mysterious mix of sobriety and joy is at the heart of a distinctively Christian sensitivity to life. Just as the community of Christ grows intent and purposeful in discipleship, so must it grow in its capacity simply to lose itself in the joy and repose of a grace-given life.

---

[15]J. Christiaan Beker, "The Passion of Sobriety," The Princeton Seminary Bulletin 5 (1984): 232-34.

[16]Benedictine Breviary, Lauds (that is, prayers at daybreak) of Tuesday, translated and quoted in Romano Guardini, The Spirit of the Liturgy, trans. Ada Lane (London: Sheed & Ward, 1930) 20.

[17]Ibid., 106.

GATHERED IN THE INCARNATION

In Jesus Christ the eternal Word of God came and lived and died in time and space. This Jesus is the human face by which God, in sovereign love, chooses to be identified. The Incarnation is his invitation to fellowship with the human community. This is the act by which he is calling us together, remaking us in Christ's image, and forming us into Christ's body.

Because Christ once entered our time, we have hope he will not despise the time we offer him in common. Because he entered the place of this world, we are bold to believe his promise that he will fill our gathering place with his presence. Only because the risen Christ mysteriously fills our time and space, only because he graciously incorporates our humanity into his body—only because Christ has done and is doing these things—do we believe our small worship gathering has any significance. Only if he prays in us can we pray. Only because he eternally utters the perfect blessing to the Father can we sing our praises. Only in the perfect self-offering of his body can we offer our bodies and our corporate life as his body. We worship, as we live, by grace alone.

All we have said about the worshiping community brings us to say one last, very direct word about Christian worship. *The Christian assembly on the Lord's Day is incomplete without the celebration of the Lord's Supper.* The sacramental nature of the church's life and worship is violated when the Eucharist is absent from the Lord's Day or when we turn our churches into little more than "sermontoriums," lecture halls, or classrooms. This must be said because, although in theory many Protestant bodies acknowledge that the true Christian liturgy involves the proclamation of the Word *and* the Eucharist, in practice the sermon continues to dominate the Sunday worship.

Without its natural association with the Lord's Supper, the Sunday sermon itself is not the event it is meant to be. It is true that whenever the Word of God is faithfully proclaimed Christ is present. But if preaching is cut off from the Lord's Supper by infrequent association, there is a danger that both preacher and congregation will fail to grasp the sacramental character of the sermon. The holding together of Word and sacrament in the wholeness of Christian worship helps to preserve the integrity of both as an invocation and celebration of Christ in our midst.

Having been addressed by Christ in the Scriptures interpreted by preaching, the community of Jesus then gathers around his table which is the sign of his self-giving. There in the God-created and human-formed bread and wine, we offer our humanity to God, as God offers Christ to us. There Jesus speaks to say, "This is my body," so that everything we are and do may be caught up into that human-divine reality which is Christ.

The Lord's Supper is not the claim of the community on the presence of Christ but the claim of that presence on the community. In the time and place of the Lord's Word and the Lord's Supper, the eyes of faith are opened to see and hear Christ renew his promise again and again, "There am I in the midst of them."

EPILOGUE

There are many ways to speak of the church, many levels of understanding. We have chosen in these pages to speak of the church in its most fundamental form and in its essential nature. Its fundamental form is the gathered local community that pursues together the life of Christian discipleship. Its essential nature is its humanity—God-given, God-touched, and ultimately God-summoned to a future only God can give. We can but make the journey in faith, live the vision in love, and go the distance in hope. This great triad of Christianity to which the missionary apostle pointed a first-century congregation is still the signpost by which the congregation today makes its pilgrimage. Out of its faith, hope, and love it invites fellow travelers into the journey.

We have further spoken of this journey as being made in the presence of Christ. This has always meant and still means Incarnation—God present in and through the human Jesus and the humanity of us all. Christian revelation at its heart is not an idea, principle, or law, but a person. Nor is the church an ideal but a sacramental reality of persons gathered in the name of Jesus Christ. In the earthly Jesus of Nazareth the fullness of God is made known in our humanity. In the resurrected Christ of Galilee the fullness of our humanity is taken to God. This is surely one of the central themes of the Christian doctrine of the Ascension. Thus the church is left with the paradox of living in both the presence and absence of Jesus. Nowhere is this paradox more clearly glimpsed than in Luke 24. Luke constructed this narrative for the church, which must live after the resurrection and ascension of Jesus. This text provides a dynamic paradigm for the Christian congregation living between the times of his going and coming. Taken as a narrative that speaks of the life of the Christian community that lives in the absence of the earthly Jesus but in the presence of the resurrected Lord, it illuminates what we have been pointing to in the pages of this book.

The story opens at dawn on the day of resurrection. It is not only the first day of the week but the first day of the new age. So shattering is the news of the resurrection that it seems to the disciples "an idle tale" (Luke 24:11). Luke then constructs a narrative of the last words and acts of Jesus that defines the relationship between the Christian community and its Lord and turns the fear and astonishment at the "idle tale" into the joy of faith and mission. Luke 24 thus speaks to the Christian congregation today of its experience of both the presence and absence of Christ—where and how we meet him, the nature of his concerns, the power of his commands, and the limitations on our desire to possess him or contain him as if he were a local deity at our control. Luke's understanding of the "exit" of Jesus (Luke 24:51) keeps modern believers from a presumptuous faith that makes the Christ little more than a puppet-god we manipulate for our hearts' desire or from a despairing faith that must blindly endure the seemingly long absence and silence of God. In either case our congregations will form their life together in light of the last words and acts of Jesus. What precisely are these?

He meets us and greets us where we are in our journey as in the story of the disciples on the Emmaus road (Luke 24:15). We may or may not be predisposed to faith, but the gospel affirms that he is concerned with our story, with our experience.

Through the *teaching of Scripture* he makes known the identity of the Messiah. The sermon of the day is rooted in Scripture (Luke 24:25-27).

He makes himself known in the *breaking of bread* (Luke 24:30-31). That Luke has in mind meeting the presence of Christ in the Lord's Supper is made unmistakable by the force of the eucharistic formula: "He took bread and blessed it and broke it and gave it to them."

He manifests *pastoral concern* for the anxiety of the disciples (Luke 24:37-38). The resurrected Lord of the church comes to his people still as the good shepherd of the soul, asking "Why are you troubled?"

Christ's presence in *table fellowship* continues to be the mark of his life with his community (Luke 24:41-43; see also John 21:9-14). The disciples had eaten together and still eat together in the shared meals of their common life.

He gives them their *mission to the world* (Luke 24:45-49). As he had called them to follow in the first word he addressed to them, he sends them to proclaim in the last word. The content of the proclamation is the heart of the gospel—the death and resurrection of the Christ and repentance and forgiveness of sins in his name. The message of Christian proclamation is itself the model for Christian pilgrimage—death and resurrection, repentance and forgiveness. The continuing process of transformation for the individual Christian and for the community will always require a willingness to die to the old order in all its manifestations of bondage. Repentance will be a constant companion on this journey. But with each death we die Christ will raise us again to life and freedom in the new order. It is the unwillingness to "lose our life" that keeps us from "finding it."

The last act that accompanies his departure is his *benediction*. He lifts his hands and *blesses his community* (Luke 24:50-51). Jesus had been through it all with his disciples. He had seen them at their best and at their worst. He had taught them, prayed with them, traveled with them. He had lived with their understandings and misunderstandings of him. He had experienced their denials, endured their pettiness, and witnessed their unfaithfulness. He had seen them follow and watched them run away. In short, he had lived in and with the totality of their humanity—their longings, disappointments, failures, fears, joy, pride—everything that made them what they were and everything that makes us what we are. His final act and final word is still that of blessing. Such is the surprise of the gospel. The Lord of the church in the hour of his departure leaves us with the blessing of his love and the promise of his presence.

This final chapter of Luke's Gospel reads virtually like an outline for the life and worship of the Christian congregation following the departure of Jesus. That he has gone away there is no doubt.

Nor is there any doubt that he has promised to meet us in all the old familiar places—as well as in many unexpected ways and unforeseen places. This is the cause for the joy of the disciples at his departure (Luke 24:52). They are now on their way in mission, having received his blessing in order to announce his blessing and to await in faith, hope, and love the consummation of history in the final benediction of redemption. Two thousand years of Christian history have not eroded the force of his promise as Christian congregations today order their life and worship in light of his postresurrection appearances. He meets us today in the same sacramental reality as he did those second and third generation Christians in congregations that sprang up in Judea, Galilee, Asia Minor, Greece, and Rome. Where two or three are gathered in his name, there he is in the midst of them.

In what way? Remember his last words and last acts that prefigure the whole course of Christian history. He meets us where we are on our journey with his life-engendering presence, using the simple, dependable, steadfast means of grace in our humanity: in the teaching of Scripture, the breaking of bread, pastoral care, table fellowship, and the missionary proclamation of the gospel. The Christian congregation that does not center its existence in the risen Lord's promise of his presence removes itself from the very source of its life and focus of its identity. But across the generations of history the risen Christ still makes himself known in the fellowship of faith, hope, and love, appearing among people on the way. Faith, hope, and love are the invigorating winds of the Spirit that have carried the Christian church across the landscape of history, renewing it in each generation while at the same time uniting each current generation with all those who have gone before and all those who are yet to come. As Reinhold Niebuhr said,

> Nothing worth doing is completed in one lifetime. Therefore we must be saved by hope. Nothing true and beautiful makes complete sense in any context of history. Therefore we must be saved

by faith. Nothing we do, no matter how virtuous, can be accomplished alone. Therefore we are saved by love.[1]

In faith we live, in love we act, in hope we wait. Such are the marks of the human church in the presence of Christ.

---

[1]Quoted in George Gilder, *Wealth and Poverty* (New York: Basic Books, 1981) 268-69.

SCRIPTURE INDEX

DATE DUE

DEMCO 38-297